Northeast Temperate Network Forest Health Monitoring Report

2006-2009

Natural Resource Report NPS/NETN/NRR—2010/206

Kate M. Miller
Northeast Temperate Network
Acadia National Park
Bar Harbor, ME 04609

Geri L. Tierney
Department of Environmental & Forest Biology
SUNY College of Environmental Science & Forestry
Syracuse, NY 13210

Brian R. Mitchell
Northeast Temperate Network
54 Elm Street
Woodstock, VT 05091

June 2010

U.S. Department of the Interior
National Park Service
Natural Resource Program Center
Fort Collins, Colorado

The National Park Service, Natural Resource Program Center publishes a range of reports that address natural resource topics of interest and applicability to a broad audience in the National Park Service and others in natural resource management, including scientists, conservation and environmental constituencies, and the public.

The Natural Resource Report Series is used to disseminate high-priority, current natural resource management information with managerial application. The series targets a general, diverse audience, and may contain NPS policy considerations or address sensitive issues of management applicability.

All manuscripts in the series receive the appropriate level of peer review to ensure that the information is scientifically credible, technically accurate, appropriately written for the intended audience, and designed and published in a professional manner. This report received informal peer review by subject-matter experts who were not directly involved in the collection, analysis, or reporting of the data. Data in this report were collected and analyzed using methods based on established, peer-reviewed protocols and were analyzed and interpreted within the guidelines of the protocols.

Views, statements, findings, conclusions, recommendations, and data in this report are those of the author(s) and do not necessarily reflect views and policies of the National Park Service, U.S. Department of the Interior. Mention of trade names or commercial products does not constitute endorsement or recommendation for use by the National Park Service.

This report is available from the Northeast Temperate Network website (http://science.nature.nps.gov/im/units/netn/) and the Natural Resource Publications Management website (http://www.nature.nps.gov/publications/NRPM).

Please cite this publication as:

NPS 962/103304, June 2010

Contents

Figures

Tables

Executive Summary

In 2006 the Northeast Temperate Network (NETN) Inventory and Monitoring Program began implementing a long-term forest monitoring program to assess status and trends in forest composition, structure and function within ten national park units: Acadia National Park (ACAD), Marsh-Billings-Rockefeller National Historical Park (MABI), Minute Man National Historical Park (MIMA), Morristown National Historical Park (MORR), Roosevelt-Vanderbilt National Historic Sites (ROVA), Saint-Gaudens National Historic Site (SAGA), Saratoga National Historical Park (SARA), and Weir Farm National Historic Site (WEFA). Roosevelt-Vanderbilt National Historic Sites includes Eleanor Roosevelt National Historic Site (ELRO), Home of Franklin D. Roosevelt National Historic Site (HOFR), and Vanderbilt Mansion National Historic Site (VAMA). To date, NETN has established and sampled 344 permanent forest plots. In 2010, NETN will begin resampling plots in ACAD, MABI, MIMA, SAGA and SARA.

This report summarizes metrics of ecological integrity for ACAD, ELRO/HOFR, MORR, VAMA, and WEFA, and examines forest composition and structure for all NETN parks sampled from 2006-2009. The ecological integrity metrics were calculated from data collected in 2007 and 2009 for ELRO/HOFR, MORR, VAMA, and WEFA and data collected from 2006-2009 for ACAD. Ecological integrity metrics include structural stage distribution, coarse woody debris (CWD) ratio, snag abundance, tree regeneration, tree condition and forest pests, invasive exotic plants and soil chemistry. Forest composition and structure summaries are based on density (stems/ha), and compare the composition of the forest canopy to the seedling and sapling strata.

Of the five parks rated herein, all except ACAD rated "Good" for forest structural stage distribution. A "Good" rating for this metric indicates that the distribution of forest successional stages is currently within the range of natural variation as we understand it. This range varies considerably across the network with much lower percentages of mature and late-successional forest expected in the oak-dominated forests of the more southern parks than in the northern hardwood and mixed forests of ACAD, MABI and SAGA. ACAD rated "Caution" overall for this metric. Given that the majority of ACAD's forests are second-growth and just beginning to reach maturity, it will be some time before ACAD can be rated "Good" for this metric.

The condition of canopy trees rated "Good" or "Caution" for all NETN parks. In most cases, "Caution" ratings were the result of higher than expected herbivory and/or chlorosis of the foliage. Hemlock woolly adelgid and elongate hemlock scale were detected on plots in ELRO/HOFR, VAMA, and WEFA, and while in route to a plot in MORR. Balsam woolly adelgid was detected in several plots in ACAD. Beech bark disease was most severe in ACAD.

Invasive species of concern were present in all the parks, though few were present in ACAD. All park subunits in ACAD were rated "Good" for this metric; indicator invasive species were only detected in one of 169 plots. Invasive species are most frequent in MORR and VAMA. Both MORR and VAMA were rated "Significant Concern," averaging over four indicator invasive species per plot. ELRO/HOFR and WEFA were not far behind, averaging roughly three indicator invasives per plot.

ROVA units rated fairly well for coarse woody debris (CWD) ratio and snag abundance. VAMA snag abundance and CWD ratio received "Good" ratings. ELRO/HOFR rated "Good" for CWD ratio and "Caution" for snag abundance. At the park level, ACAD rated "Caution" for CWD ratio and "Good" for snag abundance. MORR, WEFA and MABI were all rated "Caution" for CWD ratio, and "Significant Concern" for snag abundance.

Soil chemistry results differed between the two indicators (C:N and Ca:Al ratios), and all parks except WEFA had a "Good" rating for at least one of the ratios. Soil acidification is potentially a problem in ACAD and WEFA. Excess nitrogen may be an issue in MORR, ROVA and WEFA. Atmospheric deposition may be of greatest concern in WEFA, which rated "Significant Concern" for the C:N ratio and "Caution" for the Ca:Al ratio.

Both the ecological integrity regeneration metric and the composition and structure analyses indicate tree regeneration densities in MORR and WEFA are well below levels required to adequately restock the forest canopy, and low regeneration may also be a problem in ELRO/HOFR.

Compositional differences between the forest canopy (current forest) and seedling and sapling strata (future forest) were detected for several parks:
- Oak (*Quercus* spp.) regeneration is rare in ELRO/HOFR, MORR, SARA, VAMA, and WEFA
- Tulip poplar (*Liriodendron tulipifera*) regeneration is absent in ELRO/HOFR, MORR, VAMA, and WEFA
- Hickory (*Carya* spp.) regeneration is sparse in MORR, SARA, and WEFA
- Hemlock (*Tsuga canadensis*) regeneration is low in ELRO/HOFR and SAGA
- Beech (*Fagus grandifolia*), white ash (*Fraxinus americana*), and red maple (*Acer rubrum*) were more abundant in the seedling and sapling layers than in the canopy of ELRO/HOFR, MORR, SARA, VAMA, and WEFA

The presence of Norway maple (*Acer platanoides*) seedlings, saplings and trees in ELRO/HOFR, MIMA and VAMA is an important management concern. Norway maple can outcompete native maple species, and has the potential to replace native maples in both the understory and canopy.

These results suggest that forest conditions in most NETN parks could benefit from management actions such as reduction of white-tailed deer populations (MORR and WEFA), eradication and/or control of invasive species (all parks), and early detection of forest pests and exotic plants combined with rapid response control measures (all parks).

Acknowledgements

We would like to thank the forest monitoring field crews that have worked for us over the last 4 years including Jenna Scheub and Peter Vetere in 2006; Katie Renwick, Seth Rifkin, and Kathleen Stutzman in 2007, Jim Burka, Sophie Demaio, Lindsey Sloat, and Andrew Vincello in 2008, and Erika Gorczyca, Nikki Lightle, Andrew Vincello, and Kate Wilkin in 2009. Their hard work has made this program a success.

Introduction

The Northeast Temperate Network (NETN) of the National Park Service (NPS) Inventory and Monitoring Program developed a long-term monitoring program for forest resources in response to the identification of forest vegetation as a high-priority vital sign for the network (Mitchell et al. 2006). This program also provides data for three additional high-priority vital signs: Forest Soil Condition, White-Tailed Deer Herbivory, and Landscape Context. The overall goal of the forest monitoring program is to assess status and trends in the composition, structure, and function of NETN forested ecosystems.

Using the U.S. Forest Service's Forest Inventory and Analysis Program (FIA) as a starting point, NETN developed a protocol to monitor a representative suite of site and vegetation measures in an extensive network of randomly located permanent plots (Tierney et al. 2009b). Ten parks are monitored in this program: Acadia National Park (ACAD), Marsh-Billings-Rockefeller National Historical Park (MABI), Minute Man National Historical Park (MIMA), Morristown National Historical Park (MORR), Roosevelt-Vanderbilt National Historic Sites (ROVA), Saint-Gaudens National Historic Site (SAGA), Saratoga National Historical Park (SARA), and Weir Farm National Historic Site (WEFA) (Figure 1). Roosevelt-Vanderbilt National Historic Sites includes Eleanor Roosevelt National Historic Site (ELRO), Home of Franklin D. Roosevelt National Historic Site (HOFR), and Vanderbilt Mansion National Historic Site (VAMA).

An important goal for this program is to interpret and report condition of forest systems in a way that effectively informs park managers and other stakeholders. To facilitate reporting, NETN developed an Ecological Integrity Scorecard to be used in addition to periodic and intensive statistical analyses and reporting. The scorecard uses the concept of "ecological integrity" to interpret the condition of forested ecosystems by assessing a suite of compositional, structural, and functional metrics in relation to their natural or historical range of variation (Tierney et al., 2009a). For each metric, assessment points are defined that distinguish acceptable or expected conditions from undesired conditions based on current scientific understanding of their natural or historic range of variation (Bennetts et al. 2007). Integrity is interpreted for a broad audience using three categories: Good, Caution and Significant Concern. "Good" represents acceptable or expected conditions; "Caution" indicates a problem may exist; and "Significant Concern" indicates undesired conditions that may need management action. For some metrics, NETN does not define conditions that merit "Significant Concern" because current knowledge is insufficient to justify this rating. Ecological integrity assessment points are summarized in Table 1. For a more detailed discussion of metric justification, calculation and confidence, refer to the Ecological Integrity Reporting SOP in Tierney et al. (2009b).

NETN recognizes that "ecological integrity" may not be the primary goal of park natural resource management, particularly at historical parks and historic sites where cultural resource management may take precedence. Nevertheless, being able to compare the condition of park resources to ecological integrity benchmarks is valuable because it provides a deeper understanding of park condition, as well as a consistent baseline for assessment of management goals. NETN is willing to work with parks to develop scorecards that track progress towards park management goals that differ from ecological integrity benchmarks, in addition to reporting ecological integrity.

Table 1. Metrics and ratings for evaluating the ecological integrity of forest ecosystems.

Metric type	Metric	Metric Ranking		
		Good	Caution	Significant Concern
Landscape structure	Forest patch size	> 50 ha	10-50 ha	< 10 ha
	Anthropogenic landuse	< 10%	10 - 40%	> 40%
Structure	Structural stage	≥ 70% (MABI, SAGA), 50% (ACAD), and 25% (MIMA, MORR, ROVA, SARA and WEFA) late-successional structure	< 70% (MABI, SAGA), 50% (ACAD), and 25% (MIMA, MORR, ROVA, SARA and WEFA) late-successional structure	< 70% (MABI, SAGA), 50% (ACAD), and 25% (MIMA, MORR, ROVA, SARA and WEFA) combined mature *and* late-successional structure
	Snag abundance	> = 10% standing trees are snags and > = 10% med-lg trees are snags[1]	< 10% standing trees are snags or < 10% med-lg trees are snags	< 5 med-lg snags/ha
	Coarse woody debris ratio	> 15% live tree volume	5 - 15% live tree volume	< 5% live tree volume
Composition	Tree regeneration	Seedling ratio > = 0	Seedling ratio < 0	Stocking index outside acceptable range[2]
	Tree condition	Foliage problem < 10% *and* no priority 1 or 2 pests[3] *and* BBD ≤ 2	Foliage problem 10 - 50% *or* priority 2 pest present *or* BBD > 2	Foliage problem > 50% *or* priority 1 pest present
	Biotic homogenization	No change	Increasing homogenization	
	Indicator species: invasive exotic plants	< 0.5 key species per plot	0.5 to < 3.5 key species per plot	3.5 or more key species per plot
	Indicator species: deer browse	No decrease in frequency of most browse-sensitive species	Decrease in frequency of most browsed species *or* increase in frequency of browse-avoided species	Decrease in frequency of most browsed species *and* increase in frequency of browse-avoided species
Function	Tree growth and mortality rates	Growth ≥ 60% mean *and* Mort ≤ 1.6%	Growth < 60% mean *or* Mort > 1.6%	
	Soil chemistry: acid stress	Soil Ca:Al ratio > 4	Soil Ca:Al ratio 1 - 4	Soil Ca:Al ratio < 1
	Soil chemistry: nitrogen saturation	Soil C:N ratio > 25	Soil C:N ratio 20 - 25	Soil C:N ratio < 20

[1] Med-lg trees are ≥ 30 cm diameter-at-breast-height.
[2] Tree regeneration stocking index varies by park.
[3] Priority 1 pests are Asian longhorned beetle, emerald ash borer and sudden oak death. Priority 2 pests are hemlock woolly adelgid, balsam woolly adelgid, butternut canker, elongate hemlock scale, and beech bark disease (BBD).

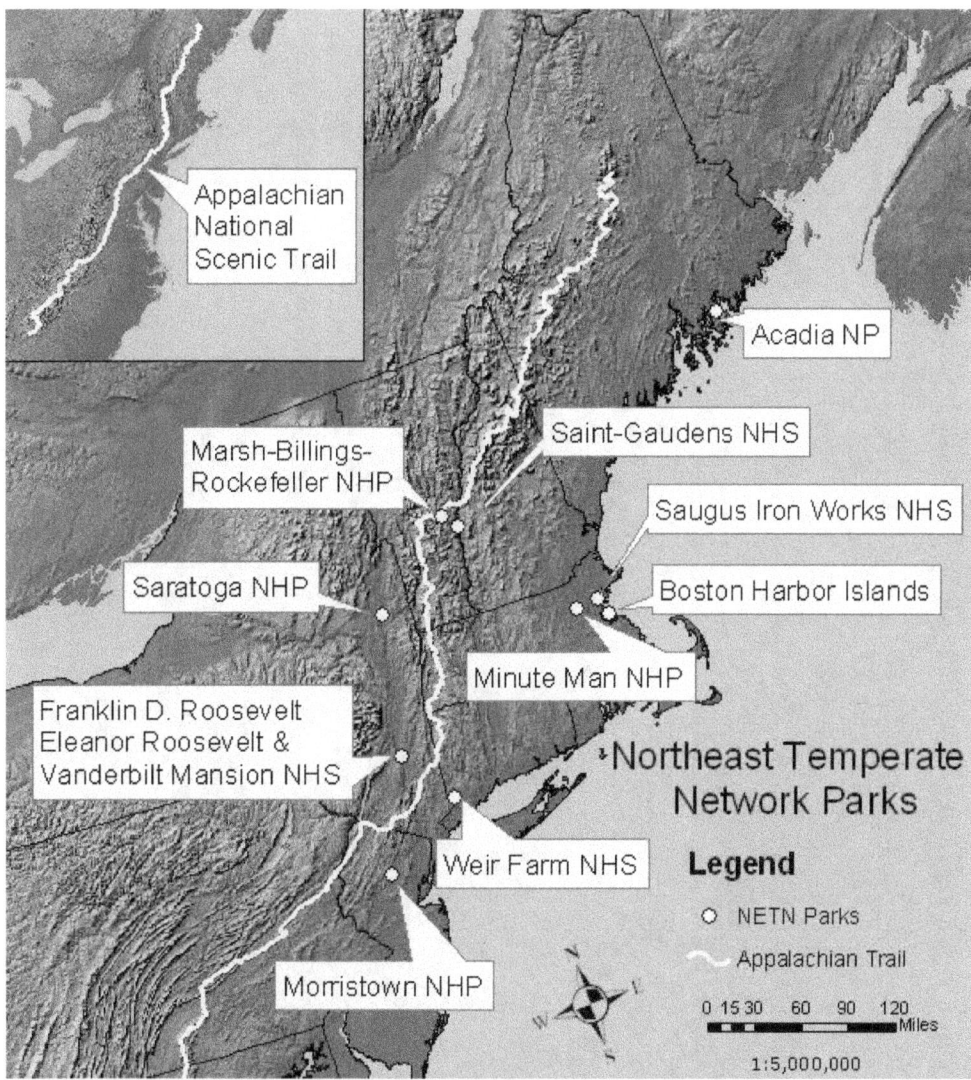

Figure 1. Map of national parks in the Northeast Temperate Network.

This report summarizes results from the onset of monitoring in 2006 through the 2009 sampling year for 344 plots installed thus far. Methods have been consistent across years for all metrics except soil sampling and regeneration, both of which were modified after the 2006 field season. Herein we report the status in ACAD, MORR, ROVA and WEFA for the following metrics: structural stage distribution, coarse woody debris and snag abundance, tree regeneration (2007-2009 only), tree condition, invasive plants, and soil chemistry. We also report on forest composition and structure for the ten sampled NETN parks using stem density (stems/ha), and compare the composition of the forest canopy to the seedling and sapling strata. These summaries provide information about the status of current forest condition and give insight into the composition of the future forest.

Methods

Permanent forest plots are installed and then sampled every 4 years using a rotating panel design. One panel is sampled each year at ACAD (four sampling panels) and in alternate years at the nine national historical parks and historic sites (two sampling panels) (Table 2). Plots were randomly located within each park using generalized random tessellation stratified sampling (GRTS; McDonald 2004). NETN has established 344 plots, and completed the first round of data collection in all parks (Table 3). Plot installation is complete at ELRO, HOFR, MABI, MIMA, MORR, SAGA, SARA, VAMA, and WEFA, and nearly complete (95% established) in ACAD. Because ELRO and HOFR are adjacent park units, the sampling design treats them as a single unit. It is not possible to report on these parks individually because the design did not provide a sufficient sample size for ELRO as a stand-alone unit. Maps of forest plot locations are included in Appendix B.

The permanent plot design is illustrated in Figure 2. Tree and stand measurements are made within fixed-area, square plots (15 x 15 m^2 at ACAD; 20 x 20 m^2 at the remaining parks). Tree regeneration is measured within three 2-m radius circular microplots embedded within each square plot. Coarse woody debris (CWD) is assessed using line intersect sampling along three 15-m transects originating at plot center. Understory diversity is monitored within eight 1-m^2 quadrats, and soil samples are obtained from a location adjacent to the plot. For a more detailed description of the forest protocol, including background information, field methods, and sample design, refer to Tierney et al. (2009b).

Table 2. Northeast Temperate Network forest monitoring panel design[1].

Panel	Year								
	1	2	3	4	5	6	7	8	9
1	X				X				X
2		X				X			
3			X				X		
4				X				X	

[1]ACAD sampled every year. SARA, MIMA, MABI, and SAGA sampled in panels 1 and 3. MORR, ROVA (HOFR, ELRO, VAMA), and WEFA sampled in panels 2 and 4.

Table 3. Northeast Temperate Network forest sampling plot allocation. Sampling intensity is the number of forested hectares per monitoring plot.

	Northeast Temperate Network Parks									
						ROVA				
	ACAD	SARA	MORR	MABI	MIMA	ELRO/ HOFR	VAMA	SAGA	WEFA	Total
Plots	176	32	28	24	20	24	16	20	10	350
Sampling Intensity (ha. forest/plot)	73	27	17	8	10	13	3	2	2	-

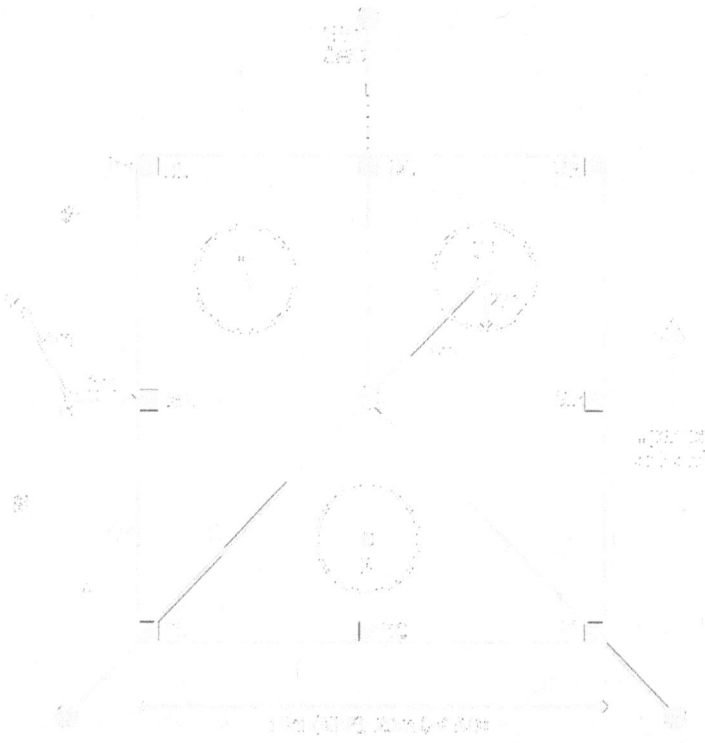

Figure 2. Plot layout showing square tree plot with three nested 2-m radius regeneration microplots, eight 1-m^2 vegetation quadrats, and three 15-m coarse woody debris (CWD) transects. S_x is location of soil sample.

Ecological Integrity Metrics

The results included in this section represent data collected from multiple years of sampling in different parks. Data for ACAD were collected in 2006, 2007, 2008, and 2009 and represent 95% of all plots that will be established in ACAD. Data for MORR, ELRO/HOFR, VAMA, and WEFA were collected in 2007 and 2009. All data were collected during the first sampling event for each plot, and represent full plot installation for all parks except ACAD.

In this section we provide a brief description of each metric and how it is calculated. For a more detailed rationale of metric selection, development, and significance, refer to the Ecological Integrity Standard Operating Procedure in NETN's Long-term Forest Monitoring Protocol (Tierney et al. 2009b). A scorecard for each park is included in Appendix A.

The following metrics are reported for ACAD, MORR, ROVA (ELRO/HOFR and VAMA), and WEFA: structural stage distribution, tree regeneration, coarse woody debris, snag abundance, tree condition, indicator invasive plants, and soil chemistry. A scorecard summarizing metric ratings for ACAD, MORR, ROVA and WEFA is included in Appendix A. Because results for these metrics were reported for MIMA, SAGA, and SARA in Miller et al. (2009), they will not be repeated here. However, we revised our metric calculations for coarse woody debris and snag abundance, and will report these metrics for all parks sampled from 2006-2009. We also separated MABI into plantation and natural forest, and report metrics for tree regeneration, coarse woody debris, and snag abundance. Most metrics are calculated on all forest and woodland plots sampled in the monitoring program. However, structural stage distribution and tree regeneration metrics were developed for forest ecosystems, and so woodland plots (i.e., plots with less than 60% canopy cover that is not due to a canopy gap) were excluded before calculating those metrics.

Structural Stage Distribution

Forested stands recovering from disturbance differ structurally from later-successional stands. The distribution of structural stages is important for maintaining a full complement of native species, which vary in their dependence upon different successional stages. Human alteration and management have greatly changed the structural stage distributions of eastern forests, and these distributions will be further affected by altered disturbance regimes coincident with global climate change and outbreaks of exotic pets and pathogens (Dale et al. 2001). Comparison of existing distributions with those expected under natural disturbance regimes provides an indicator of altered disturbance regimes as well as habitat availability.

We calculated structural stage distribution from tree size and canopy position measurements, using a method similar to that of Frelich and Lorimer (1991), but substituting basal area for exposed crown area (Goodell and Faber-Langendoen 2007). Plots are classified as pole, mature, late-successional stage or mosaic based on relative basal area of live canopy trees within pole, mature and large size classes. For all parks except ACAD, size classes are 10-25.9 cm DBH (pole), 26-45.9 cm DBH (mature) and ≥46 cm DBH (large). Dominant trees of coastal Maine (balsam fir and red spruce) are typically smaller in size than dominant trees at the other parks, and ACAD size classes have been adjusted to 10-19.9 cm DBH (pole), 20-34.9 cm DBH (mature), and ≥35 cm DBH (large). We assigned ratings based on expected percentage of late-successional forest stages across the landscape as compiled by Frelich and Lorimer (1991) and Lorimer and White (2003). Expected structural stage distributions vary among forest ecosystem types, thus assessment points vary among parks, based on the matrix forest ecosystem dominant at each park. Assessment points were based on the following matrix forest ecosystems at each park: Acadian Low-Elevation Spruce-Fir-Hardwood Forest at ACAD; both Appalachian Hemlock-Northern Hardwood Forest and Northeastern Interior Dry-Mesic Oak Forest at ELRO/HOFR and VAMA; and Northeastern Interior Dry-Mesic Oak Forest at MORR and WEFA. At parks with more than one matrix forest ecosystem type, we used the assessment points from the forest type with the lowest expected late-successional structure.

Structural stage distribution in ELRO/HOFR, MORR, VAMA, and WEFA was rated as "Good," indicating that the distribution of forest successional stages in these parks is within the range of natural variation as we understand it (Table 4). Structural stage distribution rated as "Caution" in most of ACAD, with the exception of eastern Mount Desert Island (MDI), which was scored as "Significant Concern." The "Significant Concern" rating is likely due to the young age of forests that originated after the notable fire in 1947 that swept over much of the eastern side of MDI.

While the assessment points for the dominant matrix forest in ACAD are based on work by Lorimer and White (2003) in spruce-northern hardwood forests, their age requirements for late-successional stages also correspond to the late successional stages of coastal Maine spruce/fir forest development in Davis (1961 and 1966). Davis (1961) described seven stages of spruce-fir forest development following a major disturbance (e.g., logging or fire), and considered stage 5 to be mature, and stages 6 and 7 late successional to old growth (Table 5). Comparing diameter distributions adapted from Davis 1966 with our data, it appears that most of Isle au Haut (IAH), western MDI and Schoodic Peninsula are in stage 4 to early stage 5 (Figure 3); these forests have a high density of spruce trees in the 2.5 to 10 cm DBH range, and trees over 30 cm DBH are rare to non-existent. Forests on eastern MDI are closer to stage 3 where birch and aspen species are

Table 4. Structural stage distribution of forest plots in NETN parks. MDI refers to Mount Desert Island.

Park	Subunit	Plots Sampled	% Late Succ.	% Mature & Late Succ.	Rating
ACAD	Overall	129	0.17	0.58	Caution
	Isle au Haut	11	0.10	0.70	Caution
	MDI East	57	0.14	0.39	Sig. Concern
	MDI West	56	0.23	0.72	Caution
	Schoodic	5	0.00	1.00	Caution
MABI	Natural	13	0.46	0.85	Caution
	Plantation	11	0.36	1.00	Caution
MORR		28	0.68	1.00	Good
ROVA	ELRO/HOFR	24	0.33	0.83	Good
	VAMA	16	0.69	0.94	Good
WEFA		10	0.40	0.90	Good

Table 5. Stand development stages of coastal spruce/fir forests adapted from Davis 1961.

Stage	Description
1	High proportion of paper birch following a major disturbance
2	Spruce regeneration below paper birch
3	Spruce gradually replaces birch with rapid spurts of spruce growth as birches die off
4	Spruce crowding/thicket, slowing of growth, coupled with dying suppressed saplings
5	Beginnings of moss ground cover, greater tree height (35+ feet), and spruce seedlings (mean stand age: 82 years)
6	Continued tree growth and repeated establishment of new seedlings, openings in canopy caused by death or blow-down of large trees. Development of spruce and fir saplings (mean stand age: 112 years)
7	Subsequent deaths, blow-downs, and replacement by young trees, increase in quantity of small fire, increase in overall diversification of stand age and size structure (mean stand age: 163 years)

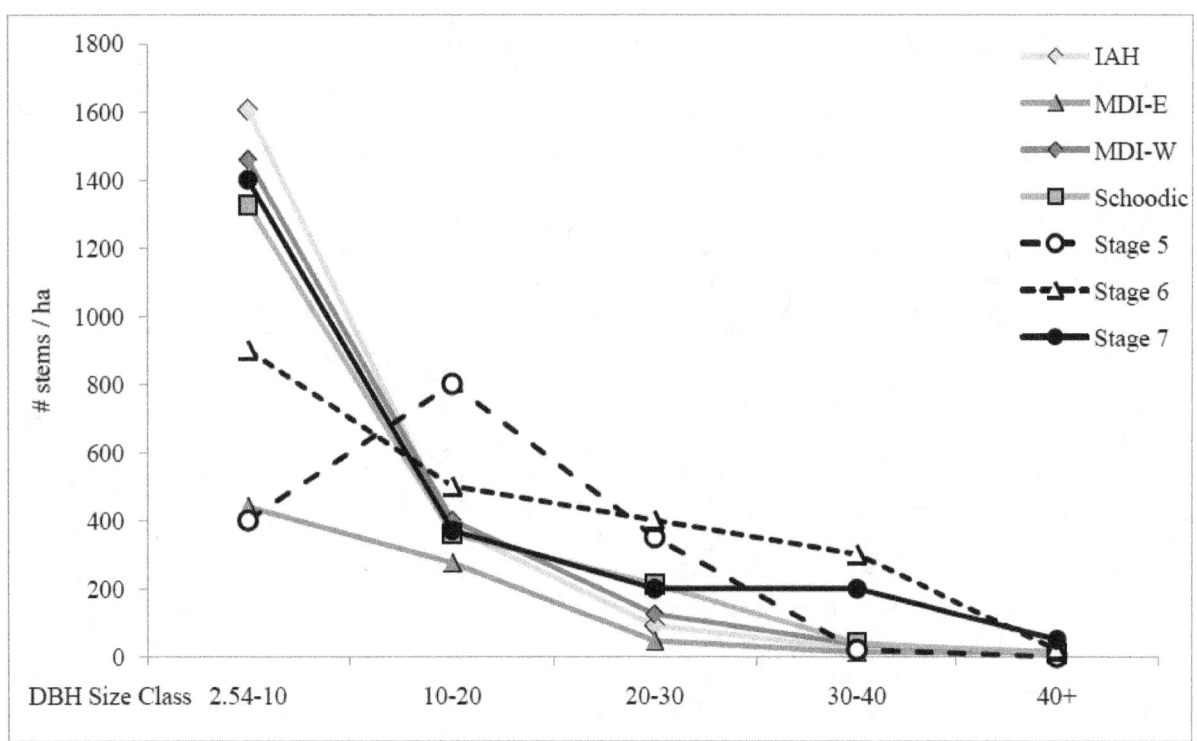

Figure 3. Diameter distribution density comparisons between Davis (1966) and NETN forest data. Stages 5-7 were adapted from Figure 5 in Davis 1966. Densities for park subunits were calculated from spruce species and balsam fir to follow the calculations in Davis (1966).

9

dying off and being replaced by spruce and fir. As long as stressors, such as invasive plants and forest pests, are kept at a minimum, the proportion of late successional forest in ACAD is expected to increase over time, thereby improving this metric rating.

Coarse Woody Debris and Snag Abundance

Dead wood, in the form of standing dead trees (snags) and fallen coarse woody debris (CWD), is an important structural feature of forests that provides habitat for many taxa. Silviculture, land management, and hazard tree removal can reduce the quantity or quality of these features. However, thoughtful land management can maintain or enhance snags and CWD (Keeton 2006).

Density of snags and volume of CWD in mature and late-successional stands vary substantially across ecosystems and with site conditions (Tyrrell et al. 1998). However, positive relationships between live and dead tree density and volume can be used to indicate expected snag and CWD levels (Tierney et al. 2009a). This metric assesses the density of snags and volume of CWD in relationship to live tree density and volume. Since NETN plots are not large enough to accurately estimate rare features such as snags, snag abundance is evaluated at the scale of the park or park subunit, and requires at least 10 plots to be adequately estimated. To facilitate comparisons of our CWD metric calculations with other studies, we report volume of CWD using metric and English units. However we have already interpreted these results for MIMA, SAGA and SARA in Miller et al. (2009), and will only discuss results for parks with new data to interpret.

ELRO/HOFR and VAMA rated fairly well for snag abundance and CWD (Table 6 and 7). VAMA rated "Good" for both metrics, whereas ELRO/HOFR rated "Caution" for snag abundance and "Good" for CWD. ELRO/HOFR missed the "Good" rating because the level of medium to large sized snags was slightly lower than the "Good" assessment point.

Table 6. Snag abundance calculations for NETN parks. Metric ratings are based on the percent of standing trees that are snags. M-L Snag refers to medium to large (≥ 30 cm DBH) diameter snags. SE refers to 1 standard error around the mean.

Park	Subunit	Metric Rating	# of Snags / ha		# of M-L Snags / ha		% of Trees as Snags	
			Mean	SE	Mean	SE	All Sizes	M-L Snags
ACAD	Overall	Good	191.5	13.2	7.9	1.6	18.1	10.1
	Isle au Haut	Good	117.0	18.7	11.7	5.7	13.1	14.3
	MDI East	Caution	169.3	19.3	5.6	1.7	17.2	8.7
	MDI West	Good	228.0	22.6	10.0	3.1	19.2	10.3
	Schoodic	n/a	291.4	58.4	4.9	4.9	26.0	10.0
MABI	Natural	Sig. Concern	36.5	12.2	3.8	2.6	7.0	2.8
	Plantation	Sig. Concern	50.0	13.1	2.3	2.3	9.6	1.0
MIMA		Sig. Concern	47.5	8.7	3.8	2.0	9.5	3.2
MORR		Sig. Concern	32.1	5.3	3.6	2.1	10.9	2.8
ROVA	ELRO/HOFR	Caution	45.8	8.1	11.5	4.8	9.5	8.0
	VAMA	Good	46.9	16.6	10.9	3.2	11.5	10.3
SAGA		Caution	90.5	17.9	10.7	4.1	13.7	5.3
SARA		Sig. Concern	82.8	17.3	3.1	1.9	17.5	3.3
WEFA		Sig. Concern	30.0	11.1	2.5	2.5	6.6	1.6

Table 7. Coarse woody debris (CWD) volume calculations for NETN parks. Metric ratings are based on the ratio of coarse woody debris volume to live tree volume and are expressed as a percent. SE refers to 1 standard error around the mean.

Park	Subunit	Metric Rating	Metric Volume (m³/ha)				English Volume (ft³/acre)				CWD Ratio (%)	
			Mean CWD	SE CWD	Mean Live Tree	SE Live Tree	Mean CWD	SE CWD	Mean Live Tree	SE Live Tree	Mean	SE
ACAD	Overall	Caution	21.4	2.4	206.2	12.6	305.3	34.6	2,947.3	180.1	14.5	3.4
	Isle au Haut	Caution	18.0	4.9	161.2	26.6	257.6	70.6	2,304.4	379.8	10.3	2.7
	MDI East	Caution	14.8	2.8	171.2	16.6	211.2	40.1	2,446.9	237.9	10.8	1.9
	MDI West	Good	32.5	5.0	271.9	22.7	464.8	71.2	3,885.7	324.6	22.0	8.9
	Schoodic	n/a	7.8	4.7	149.9	48.0	111.9	67.3	2,143.0	686.6	3.6	1.3
MABI	Natural	Caution	32.9	11.5	440.5	44.0	470.1	164.7	6,295.5	628.6	8.6	3.1
	Plantation	Caution	36.4	9.7	694.1	96.6	520.6	138.6	9,919.1	1,380.3	6.0	2.2
MIMA		Sig. Concern	8.8	2.3	330.7	58.3	125.9	32.5	4,725.6	832.9	3.1	0.7
MORR		Caution	28.7	6.3	374.5	42.3	409.7	90.2	5,352.4	605.0	8.3	1.9
ROVA	ELRO/HOFR	Good	47.8	13.9	381.4	38.3	683.5	199.0	5,450.2	546.9	26.9	13.7
	VAMA	Good	75.2	20.1	369.9	56.6	1,074.4	286.9	5,287.0	808.3	25.9	5.6
SAGA		Caution	37.7	9.3	623.5	74.5	539.2	132.6	8,910.8	1,064.1	8.3	2.7
SARA		Caution	20.7	4.7	263.9	37.4	295.6	66.4	3,771.7	534.4	13.9	5.2
WEFA		Caution	22.5	13.2	425.9	48.3	321.4	187.9	6,086.2	690.6	5.2	3.3

Overall CWD levels at ACAD were rated as "Caution." However, when the data was analyzed by subunit, the western section of MDI in ACAD rated as "Good" (Table 7). Isle au Haut and eastern MDI in ACAD fell into the "Caution" category. Schoodic Peninsula was not rated due to insufficient sample size. MORR, WEFA and MABI (both plantation and natural forest types) were rated as "Caution" for CWD volume.

When summarized across all plots, snag abundance was rated as "Good" for ACAD. This rating held up for Isle au Haut and western MDI, but eastern MDI rated as "Caution." Schoodic Peninsula was not rated for the metric due to insufficient sample size. Snag abundance was low in MABI (both plantation and natural forest types), MORR, and WEFA (Table 6).

Tree Regeneration

This metric assesses the quantity and composition of advance tree regeneration in the forest understory, which will impact future canopy structure and composition. Regeneration can be affected by a variety of stressors, including invasive species and climate change. Most notably, sustained, selective browsing by a historically high population of white-tailed deer is currently impacting seedling establishment, growth, and composition in parts of the Midwest and northeast U.S. (Cote et al. 2004). Significant impacts on forest tree regeneration are associated with deer densities ≥ 8.5 per km^2, well above pre-settlement estimates of 3-4 deer per km^2 in the northeastern U.S. (Russell et al. 2001, Augustine and deCalesta 2003).

Beginning in 2007, tree regeneration has been monitored in three 2-m radius microplots located in each forest plot. Established tree seedlings (> 15 cm tall) and saplings (1 to 10 cm dbh) are quantified by species and height class. To assess deer impacts, we use two approaches. Deer preferentially browse particular seedling species and size classes (30-75 cm tall; Cornett et al. 2000). Sweetapple and Nugent (2004) developed a simple ratio of seedling species richness in browsed versus unbrowsed size classes of preferred species. We use this ratio to distinguish "Good" from "Caution." A complementary approach by McWilliams et al. (2005) quantifies whether current seedling quantities are sufficient to restock a mid-Atlantic hardwood forest stand. We use this approach to assess minimum canopy tree stocking, which varies by park and dominant forest type. The stocking index defined in McWilliams et al. (2005) is only applicable to forest types in MORR, ELRO/HOFR, VAMA, and WEFA. Regeneration patterns in Acadian spruce/fir forests are generally a mosaic of even-aged patches, and NETN has not yet defined sufficient stocking assessment points for ACAD.

Regeneration at MORR and WEFA is well below levels required to restock the future forest (Figure 4). Heavy deer-browse pressure is likely a major cause of poor regeneration, and abundance of invasive species may be a contributing factor. Without management action to reduce deer densities and control invasive species, this pattern is likely to continue. Low regeneration at ELRO/HOFR may also be a concern, as over half of the plots sampled in ELRO/HOFR were rated as "Significant Concern."

This metric is most applicable to the parks in the southern part of NETN, and still needs to be refined to distinguish between "Caution" and "Significant Concern" for ACAD, MABI, MIMA, SAGA and SARA. Currently there do not appear to be any major issues with regeneration in ACAD or MABI. After plots in ACAD, MABI, MIMA, SAGA and SARA are resampled in 2010, we will examine regeneration trends for these parks.

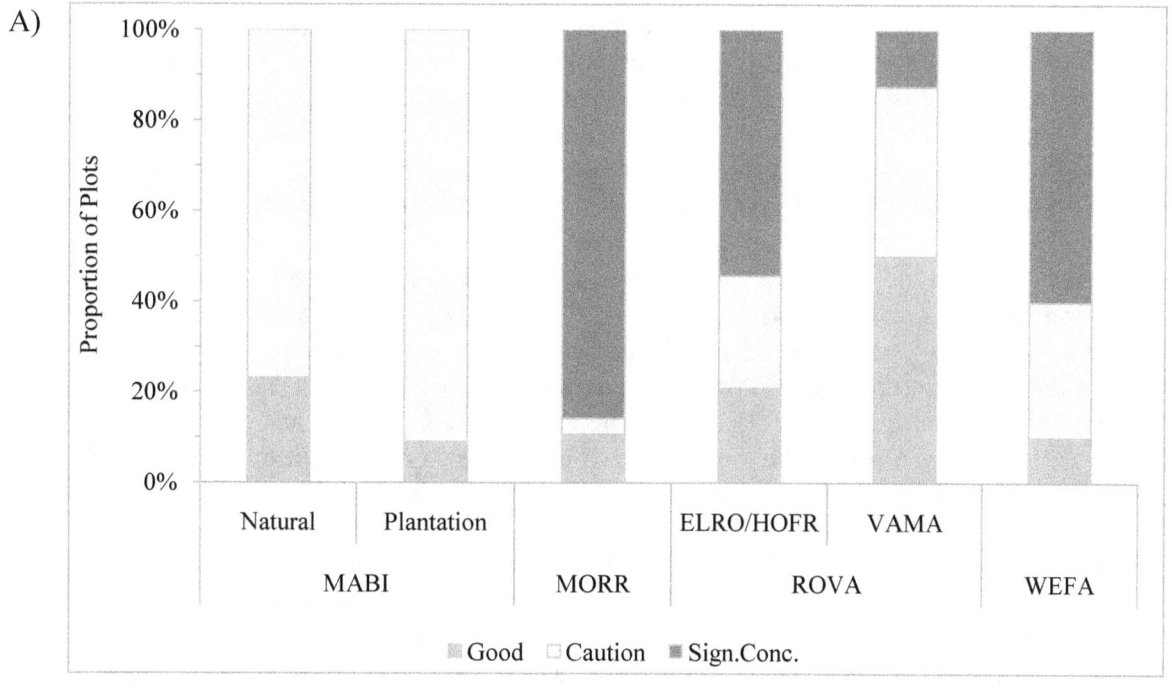

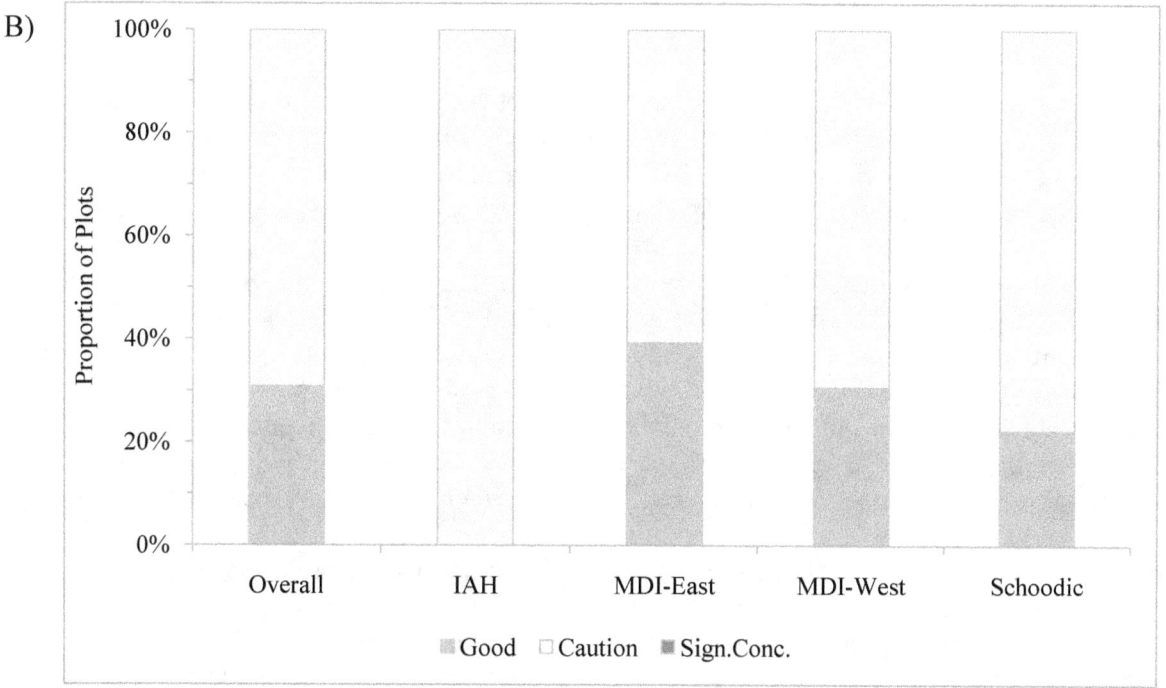

Figure 4. Proportion of plots receiving "Good", "Caution" and "Significant Concern" ratings for tree regeneration in A) national historic parks and sites, and B) ACAD overall and by subunit. Assessment points have not been established to distinguish "Caution" and "Significant Concern" for ACAD and MABI.

Tree Condition

Qualitative observations of specific tree health problems and canopy foliage condition can provide an early warning of problems or decline in canopy trees of a particular species or region. As the season progresses, most trees develop minor foliage problems. However, more extensive damage to canopy foliage may be indicative of tree health problems within a species or across a region, and could be related to soil chemistry, climate stress, pathogens, or other stressors. In particular, exotic pests and pathogens have the potential to severely impact forest tree composition as well as structure and function. A number of pest species pose serious threats to northeastern forests if they advance into the region, including Asian longhorned beetle, emerald ash borer and sudden oak death (NETN "Priority 1" pests). Other forest pests can cause problems that are not quite as severe. These NETN "Priority 2" pests include balsam woolly adelgid (BWA), beech bark disease (BBD severity > 2; heavily cracked bark with *Nectria* cankers or worse condition), butternut canker (BC), elongate hemlock scale (EHS), and hemlock woolly adelgid (HWA). To incorporate the impact forest pests have on tree condition, plots with these forest pests automatically receive a plot rating of "Caution" or worse.

Tree condition was mostly "Good" in 2009 sampled parks. Seven plots rated "Caution" in ELRO/HOFR due to the presence of HWA. HWA and EHS were also detected at one plot each in WEFA and VAMA, and were observed while navigating to a plot in MORR (HWA/EHS location is on map in Appendix B). BWA was detected in four plots on the western side of Mount Desert Island (MDI) in ACAD, and BBD was severe (i.e., BBD index > 2) in six plots on eastern MDI.

BBD is present in ELRO/HOFR, MORR, and WEFA, but the severity of the disease is very low (i.e., BBD ≤ 2); large *Nectria* cankers are rare, and there is only moderate cracking along the bark. BBD severity is much higher in ACAD. While beech trees are not very common in the park, nearly all beech trees in ACAD have large girdling *Nectria* cankers and stunted canopies.

WEFA and Isle au Haut in ACAD had the highest proportion of plots with "Significant Concern" ratings (Figure 5). The "Significant Concern" ratings in WEFA stem from two plots sampled in 2009 that are located in forested swamps, and are the result of a high percentage of necrosis and discoloring of the foliage. Summer of 2009 was fairly wet, and it's possible that the higher water tables caused stress to trees in the swamp, which resulted in foliage necrosis and chlorosis. "Caution" ratings at WEFA were primarily due to moderate levels of herbivory, and tree condition issues such as open wounds and epicormic branching (generally a sign of stress).

The "Significant Concern" ratings for Isle au Haut are from plots that are most likely forested swamps. These plots had a high prevalence of species indicative of forested swamps, including sphagnum moss, black spruce (*Picea mariana*), skunk cabbage (*Symplocarpus foetidus*), and threeseeded sedge (*Carex trisperma*). Given the high levels of stress associated with forested wetland habitats, higher levels of chlorosis and necrosis are more likely in these environments than in upland forests.

Invasive Plant Indicator Species

Invasive exotic species have the potential to impact structure, composition, and function of forested ecosystems, and are one of the leading threats to biodiversity and ecological integrity of

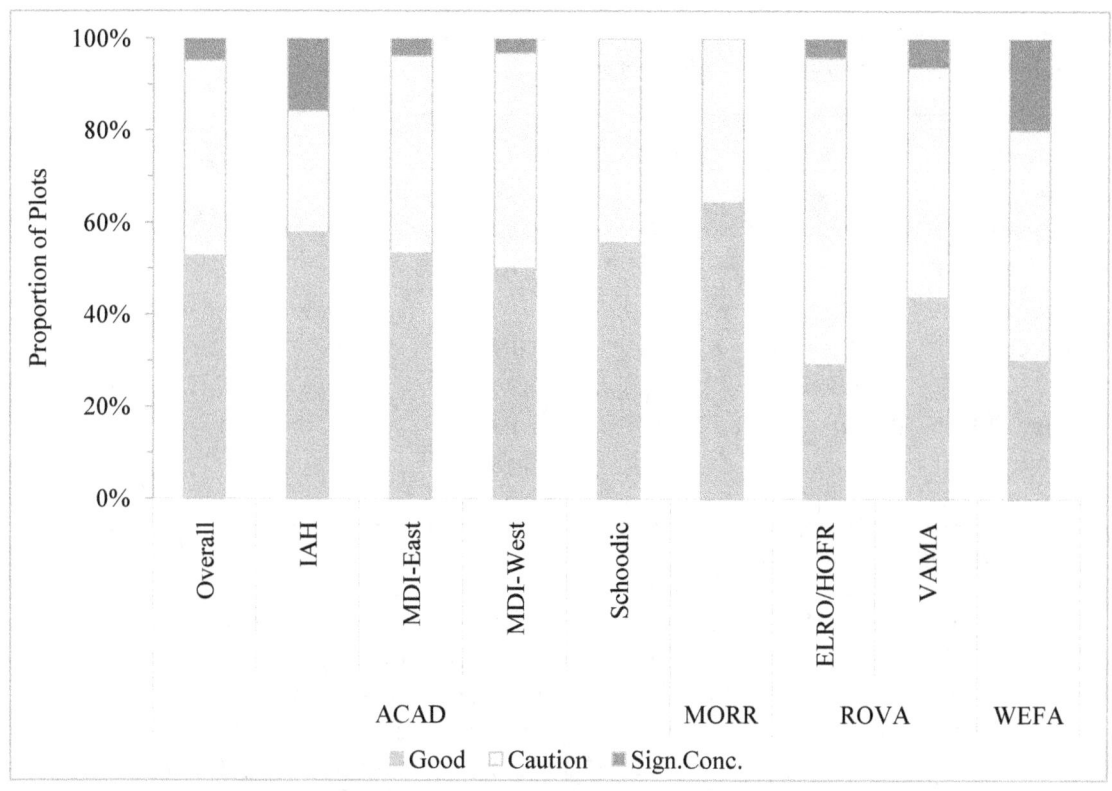

Figure 5. Proportion of plots receiving "Good", "Caution" and "Significant Concern" ratings for tree condition in ACAD, MORR, ROVA, and WEFA.

ecosystems worldwide (Mooney et al. 2005). Early detection of invasive/exotic plants is an important NETN vital sign that has been incorporated into several long-term monitoring protocols. Status and trends of invasive species are monitored on NETN forest plots, and the Eastern Rivers and Mountains Network (ERMN) and NETN are implementing a separate protocol for early detection of invasive species and forest pests.

To better understand the threat posed by invasive exotic plants, we developed a list of indicator exotic plant species that are highly invasive in northeastern forest, woodland, and successional habitats (Appendix D). Included species are those that may dominate and/or persist under shaded conditions (i.e., in forest or woodland), or that may disrupt succession to forest or woodland. Several exotic species such as knapweeds (*Centaurea* spp.) and celandine (*Chelidonium majus*) were not used as indicator species, despite being present in several parks, because they do not meet the indicator guidelines. Therefore, total abundance of exotic species is higher than reported here for indicator invasives.

ACAD rated "Good" for all park subunits; indicator invasive species have only been detected in one out of 169 plots in ACAD (Table 8). ELRO/HOFR and WEFA both fell into the "Caution" category with roughly three indicator invasive species per plot. Early detection and control of invasive species in ELRO/HOFR and WEFA should be a high management priority; without control efforts, it won't be long before ELRO/HOFR and WEFA are rated "Significant Concern."

Table 8. Indicator invasive plant species calculations for NETN parks. Metric ratings are based on the mean number of indicator invasive species found per plot.

Park	Subunit	Metric Rating	# plots	Mean # / Plot	SE[1]
ACAD	Overall	Good	169	0.02	0.01
	Isle au Haut	Good	19	0.00	0.00
	MDI East	Good	79	0.04	0.03
	MDI West	Good	62	0.00	0.00
	Schoodic	Good	9	0.00	0.00
MORR		Sig. Concern	28	5.46	0.60
ROVA	ELRO/HOFR	Caution	24	2.96	0.43
	VAMA	Sig. Concern	16	4.13	0.46
WEFA		Caution	10	3.00	0.58

[1] SE refers to 1 standard error about the mean.

MORR and VAMA were rated "Significant Concern" for invasive species, averaging more than four invasive species per plot. The most prevalent invasives in VAMA are garlic mustard (*Alliaria petiolata*), oriental bittersweet (*Celastrus orbiculatus*), tree-of-heaven (*Ailanthus altissima*), Norway maple (*Acer platanoides*), and Japanese barberry (*Berberis thunbergii*) (Table 9). The most common invasive species in MORR are Japanese barberry (*Berberis thunbergii*), Japanese stiltgrass (*Microstegium vimineum*), oriental bittersweet (*Celastrus orbiculatus*), narrowleaf bittercress (*Cardamine impatiens*), and wineberry (*Rubus phoenicolasius*). These five species each occur in over 50% of the plots in MORR, and percent cover of these species throughout the plots is high.

Soil Chemistry

NETN monitors soil chemistry to understand the effects of atmospheric deposition on the health of forest vegetation. Atmospheric deposition from rain or fog is a special concern for forests in the northeast and on thin soils where soil buffering capacity is generally low. Atmospheric deposition alters forest soil chemistry by depleting soil nutrients such as calcium (Ca), magnesium (Mg) and potassium (K) through leaching, and can result in increased availability of toxic aluminum (Al). Moreover, atmospheric deposition has dramatically increased inputs of nitrogen (N) in the northeast. Concern has arisen that excess N may "saturate" forested ecosystems, causing excess nitrification and N leaching, which in turn could exacerbate the effects of acidification (Aber et al. 1998). All these changes can reduce plant growth and increase susceptibility of trees to other stresses (Bullen and Bailey 2005).

At each plot, NETN collects a composite of up to three soil samples from each O and A horizon. If no soil horizons are apparent, NETN collects a composite of the upper soil containing fine roots to a maximum depth of 10 cm. The upper soil layers (O and A) are where the bulk of fine roots are located and plant uptake occurs. We currently rate soil chemistry based on the ratio of exchangeable Ca to Al, which has been used as an indicator of acid stress on forest soils (Cronan and Grigal 1995), and the ratio of total C to total N in soil samples, a primary indicator of N status (Aber et al. 2003, MacDonald et al. 2002). Soil metrics are rated on median values for all

Table 9. Four most frequent indicator invasive species in NETN forest plots by park.

Park	Latin name	Common Name	# Plot Occurrences[1]	% Frequency
ACAD	*Frangula alnus*	Glossy buckthorn	1	0.59
	Rosa multiflora	Multiflora rose	1	0.59
	Berberis thunbergii	Japanese barberry	1	0.59
ELRO/HOFR	*Alliaria petiolata*	Garlic mustard	8	33.33
	Ailanthus altissima	Tree-of-heaven	6	25.00
	Celastrus orbiculatus	Oriental bittersweet	5	20.83
	Berberis thunbergii	Japanese barberry	5	20.83
MORR	*Berberis thunbergii*	Japanese barberry	24	85.71
	Microstegium vimineum	Japanese stiltgrass	20	71.43
	Celastrus orbiculatus	Oriental bittersweet	19	67.86
	Cardamine impatiens	Narrowleaf bittercress	18	64.29
VAMA	*Alliaria petiolata*	Garlic mustard	15	93.75
	Celastrus orbiculatus	Oriental bittersweet	12	75.00
	Ailanthus altissima	Tree-of-heaven	9	56.25
	Berberis thunbergii	Japanese barberry	7	43.75
	Acer platanoides	Norway maple	7	43.75
WEFA	*Celastrus orbiculatus*	Oriental bittersweet	8	80.00
	Berberis thunbergii	Japanese barberry	8	80.00
	Euonymus alata	Winged burningbush	5	50.00
	Rosa multiflora	Multiflora rose	5	50.00

[1] # Plot Occurrence = the number of plots each species was found in; % Frequency = the percent of plots containing each species.

park samples (i.e., samples collected for each plot), rather than means, due to the non-normal distribution of values typical in soil chemistry sampling.

Feedback from several soil scientists in the northeast has led us to realize that these metrics are insufficient to understand the complexity of acid deposition and stress in forest soils. We plan to revise this metric to improve accuracy and interpretability. For now, we tentatively report the Ca:Al and C:N ratios, and interpret their condition collectively.

Soil chemistry results differ between the two indicators (Table 10); all parks except WEFA have a "Good" rating for at least one of the ratios. Soil acidification is potentially a problem in ACAD and WEFA. Excess Nitrogen may be issues in MORR, ROVA and WEFA. In the next round of plot sampling, NETN will resample soils to examine trends in acid deposition and stress. We hope to develop a better metric for interpreting acid stress on NETN park soils before the next round of reporting.

Table 10. Soil chemistry results for NETN parks

Park	Subunit	Median Ca:Al	Ca:Al Rating	Median C:N	C:N Rating
ACAD	Overall	1.24	Caution	32.03	Good
	Isle au Haut	1.80	Caution	34.15	Good
	MDI East	1.28	Caution	30.05	Good
	MDI West	0.91	Sig. Concern	32.48	Good
	Schoodic	1.93	Caution	39.53	Good
MORR		5.35	Good	14.34	Sig. Concern
ROVA	ELRO/HOFR	3.52	Good	16.67	Sig. Concern
	VAMA	5.94	Good	20.49	Caution
WEFA		2.10	Caution	15.31	Sig. Concern

Forest Composition and Structure

The composition and abundance of species across forest strata provide important information about the current and future forest. For each park, we estimated density of trees (≥ 10cm DBH) and saplings (1-10 cm DBH) by size class and seedlings by height class to examine compositional patterns in the forest strata. The diameter distribution and seedling density graphs that were used to assess species composition for each park are included in Appendix E and F, respectively. ACAD data were collected in 2006, 2007, 2008, and 2009 and represent 95% of all plots that will be established in ACAD. Data for MABI, MIMA, SAGA, and SARA were collected in 2006 and 2008. Data for ELRO/HOFR, MORR, VAMA, and WEFA were collected in 2007 and 2009.

Acadia National Park

Regeneration and tree diameter data were analyzed within park subunits and U.S. National Vegetation Classification Ecological System groups (Appendix E: Figures 1-3; Appendix F: Figures 1-3). We also compared patterns within and outside the 1947 fire boundary on Mount Desert Island (MDI) (Figure 6). Tree diameter distributions are typical of second-growth forests in the Acadian Region (Figure 7), with few trees represented in large diameter size classes, and many trees in smaller size classes (Kenefic et al. 2005, Solomon and Gove 1999). Seedling densities were highest on Schoodic Peninsula, though densities did not appear to be an issue across the park (Figure 8).

Figure 6. Map of Mount Desert Island and Acadia National Park (ACAD) showing extent of the 1947 fire.

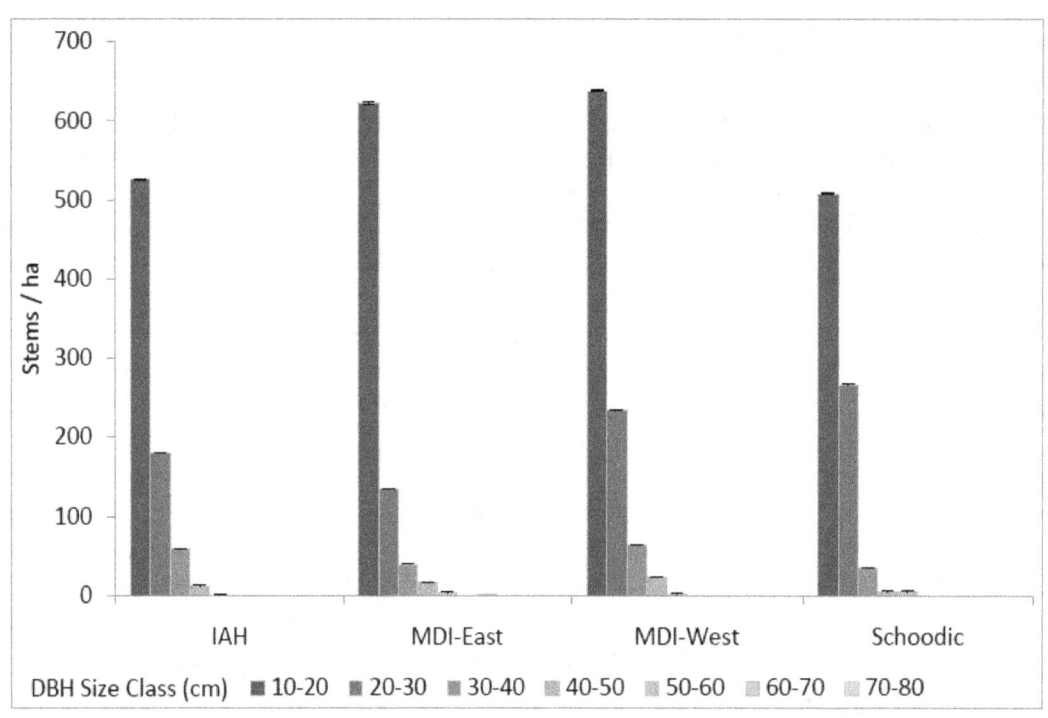

Figure 7. Tree diameter distribution in Acadia National Park by subunit. Error bars denote +1 SE about the mean.

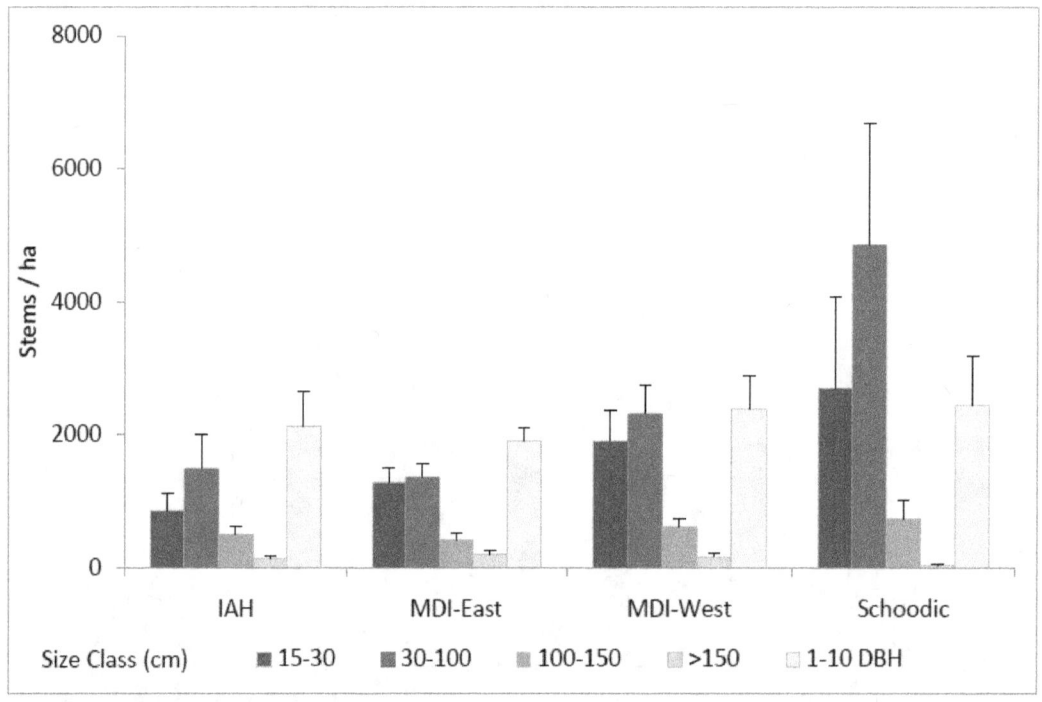

Figure 8. Density of seedlings and saplings in Acadia National Park by subunit. Classes 15-30, 30-100, 100-150, and >150 reflect seedling height (for individuals with diameter at breast height <1), and 1-10 DBH reflects sapling diameter at breast height. Error bars denote +1 SE about the mean.

Species composition of the regeneration layer (i.e., seedlings and saplings) on MDI is similar to that of the canopy. One exception is the eastern portion of MDI within the boundary of the 1947 fire that burned over 3,500 ha of the park (Figure 6). Nearly half of the area burned was stand replacing (i.e., the disturbance wiped out most or all of the existing forest), and the early-successional species big tooth aspen (*Populus grandidentata*) and birch species (*Betula papyrifera* and *B. populifolia*) were the first to occupy the canopy post-fire (Barnicle 1984). As is expected, these stands appear to be shifting to later successional forest species, with white ash (*Fraxinus americana*), northern red oak (*Quercus rubra*), red maple (*Acer rubrum*) and striped maple (*Acer pensylvanicum*) occurring at higher seedling densities than big tooth aspen (*Populus grandidentata*) and trembling aspen (*P. tremuloides*). Aspen and birch species are the most abundant standing dead trees in the burned area, further suggesting a shift to later successional forests. This pattern is most evident in the Boreal Aspen-Birch Forest Ecological System, which only occurs in the park within the boundary of the 1947 fire.

The seedling layer on Isle au Haut (IAH) is almost entirely dominated by red spruce (*Picea rubens*) and black spruce (*Picea mariana*); other canopy species, such as red maple (*Acer rubrum*), yellow birch (*Betula alleghaniensis*) and pine species (*Pinus strobus, P. banksiana and P. rigida*) were not present in the understory. Patterns are similar, but less extreme on Schoodic Peninsula.

Marsh-Billings-Rockefeller National Historical Park

Regeneration (i.e., seedlings and saplings) and tree diameter data were analyzed separately for plantations and natural forest stands because the different management strategies in these areas are likely to influence composition and density (Appendix E: Figure 4, Appendix F: Figure 4). Natural forests appear to follow the reverse-J curve in distribution, while plantations are more consistent with the rotated sigmoid distribution (which includes a plateau or hump of mid-sized trees) (Gove et al. 2008). Both distributions are found under natural forest management, though the latter is also associated with disturbed conditions. The Structural Complexity Enhancement (SCE) management approach devised by Keeton (2006), which aims to promote late-successional characteristics in northern hardwood stands, uses the rotated sigmoid distribution as a harvesting guide to allocate more growing space to larger size classes. If not already in practice, the SCE approach would be a useful guide for forest management in MABI. Other SCE objectives that would benefit managed forests in MABI include increasing abundance of coarse woody debris and standing dead trees, adding vertical structure and increasing variability of horizontal density.

Composition of regeneration differs between the two management types. The regeneration in naturally regenerated forests is more diverse than in plantations, and closely resembles the composition of the forest canopy. In plantations, ash (*Fraxinus* spp.) seedlings dominate the regeneration layer, and seedlings over 1 m in height are infrequent. Few of the non-native plantation species are present in the regeneration layer, indicating that naturalization rates are low. The exception may be Norway spruce (*Picea abies*), which is present in small amounts in the understory.

21

Minute Man National Historical Park

In this park, most of the dominant species that make up the forest canopy are also present in the regeneration (i.e., seedling and sapling) layer (Appendix E: Figure 5, Appendix F: Figure 5). An important concern is the presence of non-native tree species, especially Norway maple (*Acer platanoides*) and black locust (*Robinia pseudoacadia*), in both the regeneration and canopy layers. Norway maple is fast growing, extremely shade tolerant and a prolific seed producer, and outcompetes native maple species (Martin 1999). If not controlled by management, this species may replace sugar maple (*Acer saccharum*) and red maple (*Acer rubrum*) as the dominant maple species in the richer sites in the park. Black locust may pose less of a threat than Norway maple, because the species is short-lived and not able to regenerate in shade. However, Von Holle et al. (2005) documented higher abundance and diversity of invasive species growing under a black locust canopy than a canopy composed of native species.

Morristown National Historical Park

The tree diameter distribution in MORR reveals a diverse forest canopy composed of beech (*Fagus grandifolia*), tulip poplar (*Liriodendron tulipifera*), and several species of maple (*Acer* spp.), birch (*Betula* spp.), hickory (*Carya* spp.), oak (*Quercus* spp.), and ash (*Fraxinus* spp.) (Appendix E: Figure 6, Appendix F: Figure 6). However, a comparison of tree density by size class across all NETN parks shows MORR to have the lowest density of trees 10-30 cm DBH (Figure 9). It is likely that the low density of saplings and young trees in MORR is the result of long-term deer browse pressure suppressing forest regeneration.

As discussed in the EI Scorecard section on regeneration, seedling and sapling densities are well below levels required to adequately restock the forest canopy (Figure 10), and except for beech, all other dominant canopy species are rare to absent in the regeneration layer. Continued deer browse pressure is likely to result in a compositional shift in the canopy towards beech, and possibly a sparser canopy if widespread failure of forest regeneration continues (Rooney and Waller 2003). If beech bark disease becomes more severe in the park, then even more dramatic changes may occur to the composition and structure of the forest canopy.

Roosevelt-Vanderbilt National Historic Sites

In both VAMA and ELRO/HOFR, many of the dominant canopy species are also present in the regeneration (i.e., seedling and sapling) layer, with the exception of eastern hemlock (*Tsuga canadensis*) (Appendix E: Figure 7, Appendix F: Figure 7). Eastern hemlock is the second most common tree species (based on stem density) in ELRO/HOFR and third most common in VAMA. However, no eastern hemlock seedlings and only a few saplings were observed in the 40 plots located throughout ELRO, HOFR and VAMA.

VAMA has the highest density of small seedlings (15-30 and 30-100 cm height classes) of any park unit in NETN (Figure 10). The vast majority of the seedlings were sugar maple (*Acer saccharum*) and black maple (*Acer nigrum*). The dense seedling layer in VAMA is consistent with the dense seedling banks common in mesic northern hardwood forests. However, the presence of Norway maple (*Acer platanoides*) in the understory is an important concern. While Norway maple is currently uncommon in the canopy, it has the potential to replace native maple species in the understory and ultimately the canopy (Martin 1999). Two additional invasive trees species, tree-of-heaven (*Ailanthus altissima*) and black locust (*Robinia pseudoacacia*), were also

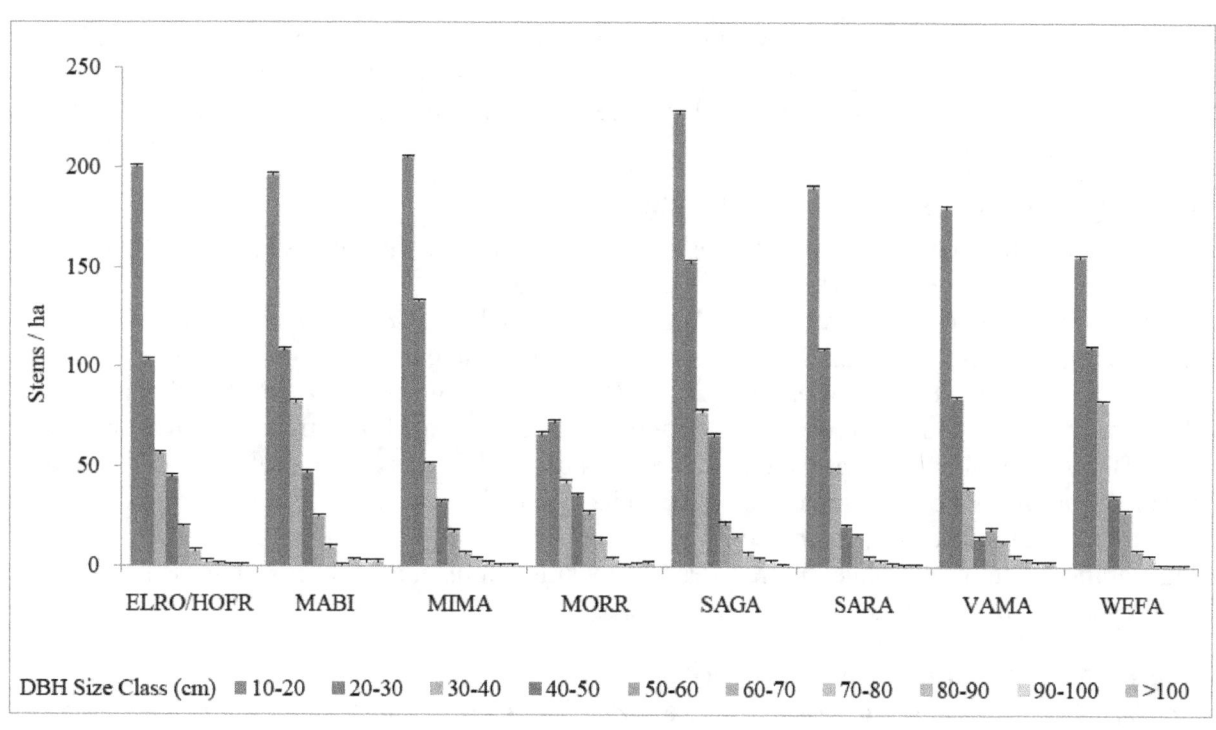

Figure 9. Tree diameter distribution of forest plots in NETN national historic parks and sites. Error bars denote +1 SE about the mean.

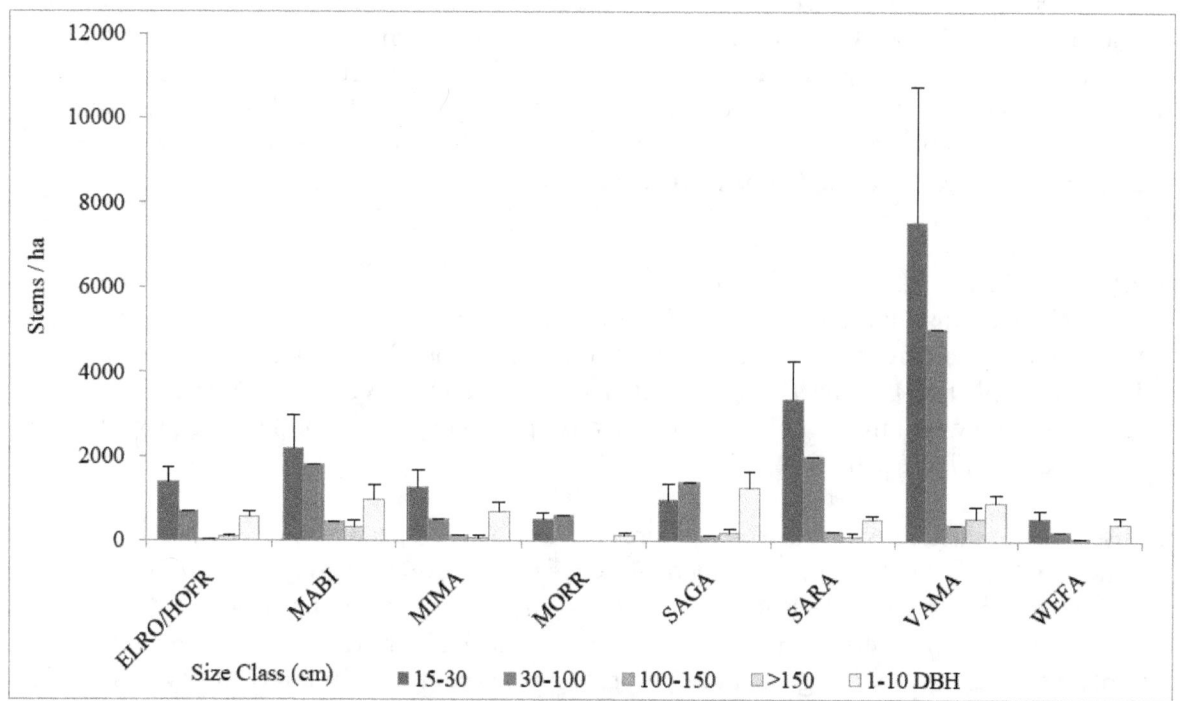

Figure 10. Density of seedlings and saplings in NETN national historical parks and historic sites. Classes 15-30, 30-100, 100-150, and > 150 reflect seedling height (for individuals with diameter at breast height < 1), and 1-10 DBH reflects sapling diameter at breast height. Error bars denote +1 SE about the mean.

23

present in the understory and canopy, but were not nearly as prevalent as Norway maple. While the density of maple seedlings in ELRO/HOFR is considerably less than VAMA, composition and density patterns are similar for non-maple seedlings, and Norway maple and tree-of-heaven are also an important concern.

Saint-Gaudens National Historic Site

At SAGA, the tree diameter distribution is typical of second-growth forests in central New England (Figure 9), with few trees represented in large diameter size classes, and many trees in smaller size classes (D'Amato et al. 2008). Eastern hemlock (*Tsuga canadensis*) was the dominant tree species in SAGA forest plots, but eastern hemlock seedlings were sparse (Appendix E: Figure 8, Appendix F: Figure 8). Beech (*Fagus grandifolia*) was by far the dominant species in both the seedling and sapling strata, but most beech trees were less than 20 cm DBH. A similar pattern has been observed in hardwood forests in the northeastern U.S. here a century or more of beech bark disease (BBD) has yielded thickets of beech that originated from prolific root sprouting by stressed and dying trees (Shigo 1972, Griffin et al. 2003). If regeneration patterns continue, future forest composition could shift towards increased dominance of BBD damaged beech and less eastern hemlock.

Saratoga National Historical Park

Tree species composition in SARA is typical of the forests in the northeastern U.S. that regenerated from old fields following agricultural abandonment, which tend to be dominated by white pine (*Pinus strobus*), red maple (*Acer rubrum*), and white ash (*Fraxinus americana*) (Flinn et al. 2005, Foster 1992). Density of seedlings less than 1m tall is relatively high (Figure 10), and is dominated by ash species (primarily *Fraxinus americana*). Other important canopy species such as oak (*Quercus* spp.) and hickory (*Carya* spp.) are underrepresented as seedlings and saplings (Appendix E: Figure 9, Appendix F: Figure 9). If this pattern continues, the resulting future forest may become even more dominated by ash and red maple, and have a smaller component oak and hickory species. White pine is also underrepresented in the regeneration layer as compared to the canopy; this is to be expected as successional forests at this park mature.

Weir Farm National Historic Site

The tree diameter distribution is typical of second-growth forests in the northeast with few large-diameter trees and many trees in small diameter classes (Figure 9). Dominant canopy species include red maple (*Acer rubrum*), sugar maple (*Acer saccharum*), yellow birch (*Betula alleghaniensis*), sweet birch (*Betula lenta*), and oak species (*Quercus* spp.) (Appendix E: Figure 10, Appendix F: Figure 10).

As discussed in the Ecological Integrity Scorecard section on regeneration, seedling and sapling densities are below levels required to adequately restock the forest canopy (Figure 10). Continued and/or increased deer browse pressure could result in a compositional shift in the canopy towards non-preferred browse species such as black cherry (*Prunus serotina*), and possibly a sparser canopy if regeneration of forest species continues to fail (Rooney and Waller 2003).

Management Implications

Acadia National Park

Forest condition, composition and structure vary across ACAD subunits, but in general species composition and structure are typical of second growth forests in the Acadian region. Structural stage distribution, coarse woody debris and snag abundance ratings were lowest in the eastern section of Mount Desert Island (MDI). The "Caution" and "Significant Concern" ratings on eastern MDI are all likely the result of the 1947 fire. Spruce (primarily red spruce) and balsam fir are replacing the birch and aspen dominated forests that originated after the fire on eastern MDI. While it may appear that coarse woody debris and snags are abundant in these forests due to dying birch and aspen, these trees often do not meet the size requirement (i.e., $\geq$ 10cm diameter) to be included in the metric calculations. Forests on Isle au Haut, Schoodic Peninsula, and western MDI are in the early stages of stand maturity, and it will be some time before they develop late-successional structure sufficient to receive a "Good" rating for the structural stage distribution metric. As long as management efforts keep threats such as invasive plant species and forest pests at a minimum, these metrics are expected to improve over time throughout the park.

Morristown National Historical Park

An overabundance of white-tailed deer and invasive species are significantly impacting forest health in MORR and management action will be necessary to improve this situation. Invasive species are pervasive throughout MORR, averaging over five key invasive species per plot and comprising most of the plant cover in the understory. Regeneration densities are well below levels required to restock the future forest, and have been for some time as evidenced by the lower than expected density of trees in the 10-30 cm size classes. White-tailed deer management and control of invasive species will likely need to be performed in unison to improve regeneration densities and native understory diversity. In areas where seed sources are absent, planting of native tree seedlings may be necessary to improve forest regeneration.

Roosevelt-Vanderbilt National Historic Sites

Forest condition, composition and structure vary considerably between ELRO/HOFR and VAMA. VAMA has the highest average density of seedlings in NETN, whereas ELRO/HOFR was rated as "Significant Concern" for regeneration. Invasive species and forest pests are an issue in both ELRO/HOFR and VAMA. Control and early detection of invasive species and forest pests should be a high priority for all ROVA units. Eradicating invasive tree species, such as Norway maple (*Acer platanoides*) and tree-of-heaven (*Ailanthus altissima*), is particularly important for ensuring forest health in ELRO/HOFR and VAMA.

Weir Farm National Historic Site

Forest health appears to be impacted by a number of factors, including white-tailed deer herbivory, forest pests, invasive species, poor soil chemistry, and lack of dead wood in the form of snags and coarse woody debris. Coarse woody debris and snag abundance are expected to increase over time as WEFA's second-growth forests mature. Therefore, we suggest management efforts to improve forest health in WEFA should focus on controlling invasive species and reducing deer densities. Early detection of new invasive species and forest pests should also be a priority in the park.

Conclusions

The first round of data collection indicates several factors that appear to be impacting forest health throughout NETN parks, including white-tailed deer herbivory, invasive species, forest pests, acid deposition, and lack of dead wood in the form of coarse woody debris and snags. Early detection and eradication of key forest pests and invasive exotic plant species should be a priority at all NETN parks. In addition, control of existing invasive species populations, increased retention of CWD and snags, and reduction of white-tailed deer populations are advisable at several parks. As the impacts of climate change and other regional stressors increasingly challenge long-term management of park resources, it becomes even more important to limit the impacts of local stressors, and to respond with active management.

Literature Cited

Aber, J., W. McDowell, K. Nadelhoffer, A. Magill, G. Berntson, M. Kamakea, S. McNulty, W. Currie, L. Rustad, and I. Fernandez. 1998. Nitrogen saturation in temperate forest ecosystems. BioScience 48:921-934.

Aber, J., C. Goodale, S. Ollinger, M. L. Smith, A. Magill, M. Martin, R. Hallett, and J. Stoddard. 2003. Is nitrogen deposition altering the nitrogen status of northeastern forests? BioScience 53:375-389.

Augustine, D. J. and D. deCalesta. 2003. Defining deer overabundance and threats to forest communities: From individual plants to landscape structure. Ecoscience 10:472-486.

Barnicle, K. 1984. Impacts of the 1947 fire and the post-fire salvage operations on the vegetation of Acadia National Park. University of Massachusetts, Amherst, Massachusetts. 28 pp.

Bennetts R. E., J. E. Gross, K. Cahill, C. McIntyre, B. B. Bingham, A. Hubbard, L. Cameron, and S. L. Carter. 2007. Linking monitoring to management and planning: assessment points as a generalized approach. The George Wright Forum 24:59–77.

Bullen, T., and S. Bailey. 2005. Identifying calcium sources at an acid deposition-impacted spruce forest: a strontium isotope, alkaline earth element multi-tracer approach. Biogeochemistry 74:63-99.

Cote, S. D., T. P. Rooney, J. P. Tremblay, C. Dussault, and D. M. Waller. 2004. Ecological impacts of deer overabundance. Annual Review of Ecology Evolution and Systematics 35:113-147.

Cronan, C. S. and D. F. Grigal. 1995. Use of calcium/aluminum ratios as indicators of stress in forest ecosystems. Journal of Environmental Quality 24:209-226.

Dale, V. H., L. A. Joyce, S. McNulty, R. Neilson, M. Ayres, M. Flannigan, P. Hanson, L. Irland, A. Luge, C. Peterson, *and others*. 2001. Climate change and forest disturbances. BioScience 51:723-734.

D'Amato, A. W., D. A. Orwig, and D. R. Foster. 2008. The influence of successional processes and disturbance on the structure of *Tsuga canadensis* forests. Ecological Applications 18: 1182-1199.

Davis, R. B. 1961. The spruce-fir forests of the coast of Maine. Ph.D. thesis. Cornell University, Ithaca, New York. 307 pp.

Davis, R. B. 1966. Spruce-fir forests of the coast of Maine. Ecological Monographs 36:80-94.

Flinn, K. M., M. Vellend, and P. L. Marks. 2005. Environmental causes and consequences of forest clearance and agricultural abandonment in central New York, USA. Journal of Biogeography 32:439-452

Foster, D. R. 1992. Land-use history (1730-1990) and vegetation dynamics in Central New England, USA. Journal of Ecology 80:753-771.

Frelich, L. E. and C. G. Lorimer. 1991. Natural disturbance regimes in hemlock-hardwood forests of the upper Great Lakes Region. Ecological Monographs. 61:145-164.

Goodell, L. and D. Faber-Langendoen. 2007. Development of stand structural stage indices to characterize forest condition in upstate New York. Forest Ecology and Management 249:158-170.

Gove, J. H., M. J. Ducey, W. B. Leak, and L. Zhang. 2008. Rotated sigmoid structures in managed uneven-aged northern hardwood stands: a look at the Blur Type III distribution. Forestry 81: 161-176.

Griffin, J. M., G. M. Lovett, M. A. Arthur, and K. C. Weathers. 2003. The distribution and severity of beech bark disease in the Catskill Mountains, N.Y. Canadian Journal of Forest Research 33:1754-1760.

Keeton, W. S. 2006. Managing for late-successional/old-growth characteristics in northern hardwood-conifer forests. Forest Ecology and Management 235:129-142.

Kenefic, L. S., A. S. White, A. R. Cutko, and S. Fraver. 2005. Reference stands for silvicultural research: a Maine perspective. Journal of Forestry 103: 363-367.

Lorimer, C. G., and A. S. White. 2003. Scale and frequency of natural disturbances in the northeastern US: implications for early successional forest habitats and regional age distributions. Forest Ecology and Management 185:41-64.

MacDonald, J. A., N. B. Dise, E. Matzner, M. Armbruster, P. Gundersen, and M. Forsius. 2002. Nitrogen input together with ecosystem nitrogen enrichment predict nitrate leaching from European forests. Global Change Biology 8:1028-1033.

Martin, P. H. 1999. Norway maple (*Acer platanoides*) invasion of a natural forest stand: understory consequence and regeneration patterns. Biological Invasions 1:215-222.

McDonald, T. L. 2004. GRTS for the average Joe: a GRTS sampler for Windows. http://www.west-inc.com/biometrics_reports.php. Accessed 14 May 2010.

McWilliams, W. H., T. W. Bowersox, P. H. Brose, and others. 2005. Measuring tree seedlings and associated understory vegetation in Pennsylvania's forests. Pages 21-26 *in* R. E. McRoberts, G. A. Reams, P. C. Van Deusen, and others. editors. Proceedings of the Fourth

Annual Forest Inventory and Analysis Symposium. General Technical Report NC-252. U.S. Forest Service, North Central Research Station, St. Paul, Minnesota.

Miller, K. M., G. L. Tierney, and B. R. Mitchell. 2009. Northeast Temperate Network 2006-2008 forest health monitoring report. Natural Resource Report NPS/NETN/NRR— 2009/104. National Park Service, Fort Collins, Colorado.

Mitchell B. R., W. G. Shriver, F. Dieffenbach, T. Moore, D. Faber-Langendoen, G. Tierney, P. Lombard, and J. Gibbs. 2006. Northeast Temperate Network vital signs monitoring plan. Technical Report NPS/NER/NRTR--2006/059. Naitonal Park Service, Northeast Temperate Network, Woodstock, Vermont. (http://science.nature.nps.gov/im/units/NETN/monitor/monitor.cfm). Accessed 14 May 2010.

Mooney, H., R. Mack, J. McNeeley, L. Neville, P. Schei, and J. Waage. 2005. Invasive alien species: a new synthesis. Island Press, Washington, DC.

Rooney, T. P. and D. M. Waller. 2003. Direct and indirect effects of white-tailed deer in forest ecosystems. Forest Ecology and Management 181:165-176.

Russell, F. L., D. B. Zippin, and N. L. Fowler. 2001. Effects of white-tailed deer (*Odocoileus virginianus*) on plants, plant populations, and communities: a review. American Midland Naturalist 146:1-26.

Shigo, A. L. 1972. The beech bark disease today in the Northeastern U.S. Journal of Forestry 70:286-289.

Solomon, D. S., and J. H. Gove. 1999. Effects of uneven-age management intensity on structural diversity in two major forest types in New England. Forest Ecology and Management 114: 265-274.

Sweetapple, P. J., and G. Nugent. 2004. Seedling ratios: a simple method for assessing ungulate impacts on forest understories. Wildlife Society Bulletin 32:137-147.

Tierney, G., D. Faber-Langendoen, B. Mitchell, W. G. Shriver, and J. Gibbs. 2009a. Monitoring and evaluating the ecological integrity of forest ecosystems. Frontiers in Ecology and the Environment 7, doi: 10.1890/070176.

Tierney, G., B. Mitchell, K. Miller, J. Comiskey, A. Kozlowski, and D. Faber-Langendoen. 2009b. Long-term forest monitoring protocol: Northeast Temperate Network. Natural Resource Report NPS/NETN/NRR—2009/117. National Park Service, Fort Collins, Colorado.

Tyrrell, L. E., G. J. Nowacki, D. S. Buckley, E. A. Nauertz, J. N. Niese, J. L. Rollinger, T. S. Crow, and J. C. Zasada. 1998. Information about old growth for selected forest type groups in the eastern United States. General Technical Report. NC-197. U.S. Forest Service, St. Paul, Minnesota.

Appendix A. Ecological Integrity Scorecard for NETN parks; selected metrics are based on the initial round of data collection (2006-2009).

Park	Subunit	Structural Stage Distribution	Coarse Woody Debris[1]	Snag Abundance[2]	Tree Regeneration[3]	Tree Condition/ Forest Pests	Invasive Plants	Soil Ca:Al	Soil C:N
ACAD	Overall	Caution	Caution	Good	---	Good	Good	Caution	Good
	Isle au Haut	Caution	Caution	Good	---	Caution	Good	Caution	Good
	MDI East	Sig.Conc.	Caution	Caution	---	Good	Good	Caution	Good
	MDI West	Caution	Good	Good	---	Good	Good	Sig.Conc.	Good
	Schoodic	Caution	---	---	---	Good	Good	Good	Good
MORR		Good	Caution	Sig.Conc.	Sig.Conc.	Good	Sig.Conc.	Good	Sig.Conc.
ROVA	ELRO/HOFR	Good	Good	Caution	Sig.Conc.	Caution	Caution	Good	Sig.Conc.
	VAMA	Good	Good	Good	Good	Caution	Sig.Conc.	Good	Caution
WEFA		Good	Caution	Sig.Conc.	Sig.Conc.	Caution	Caution	Caution	Sig.Conc.

[1] The coarse woody debris metric was not rated for Schoodic Peninsula due to insufficient sample size.
[2] The snag abundance metric was not rated for Schoodic Peninsula due to insufficient sample size.
[3] Tree regeneration metric is not appropriate for spruce/fir forests in ACAD.

33

Appendix B. Forest plot locations in ACAD, MORR, ROVA and WEFA

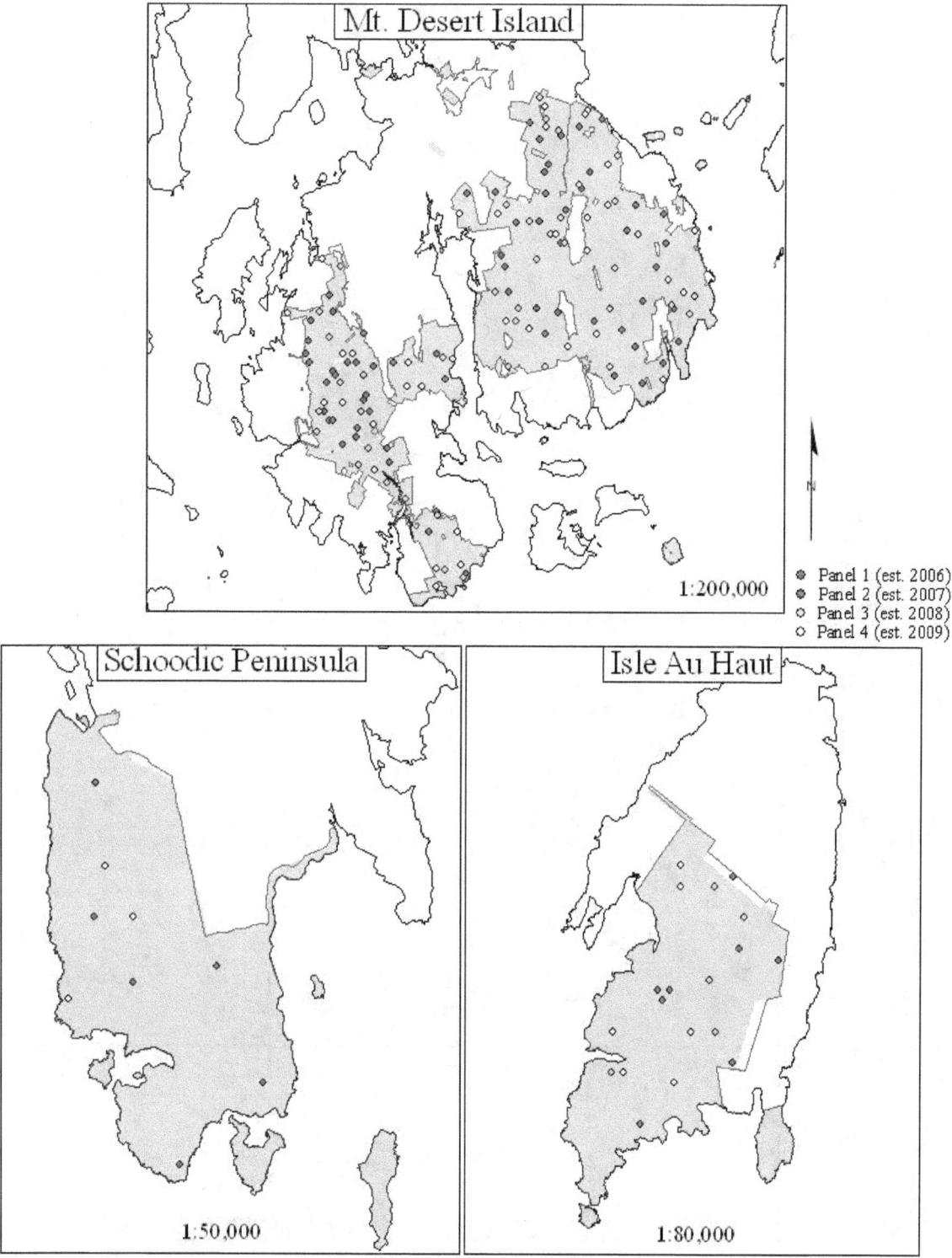

Figure B-1. Forest plot locations in Acadia National Park representing 4 years of plot establishment.

35

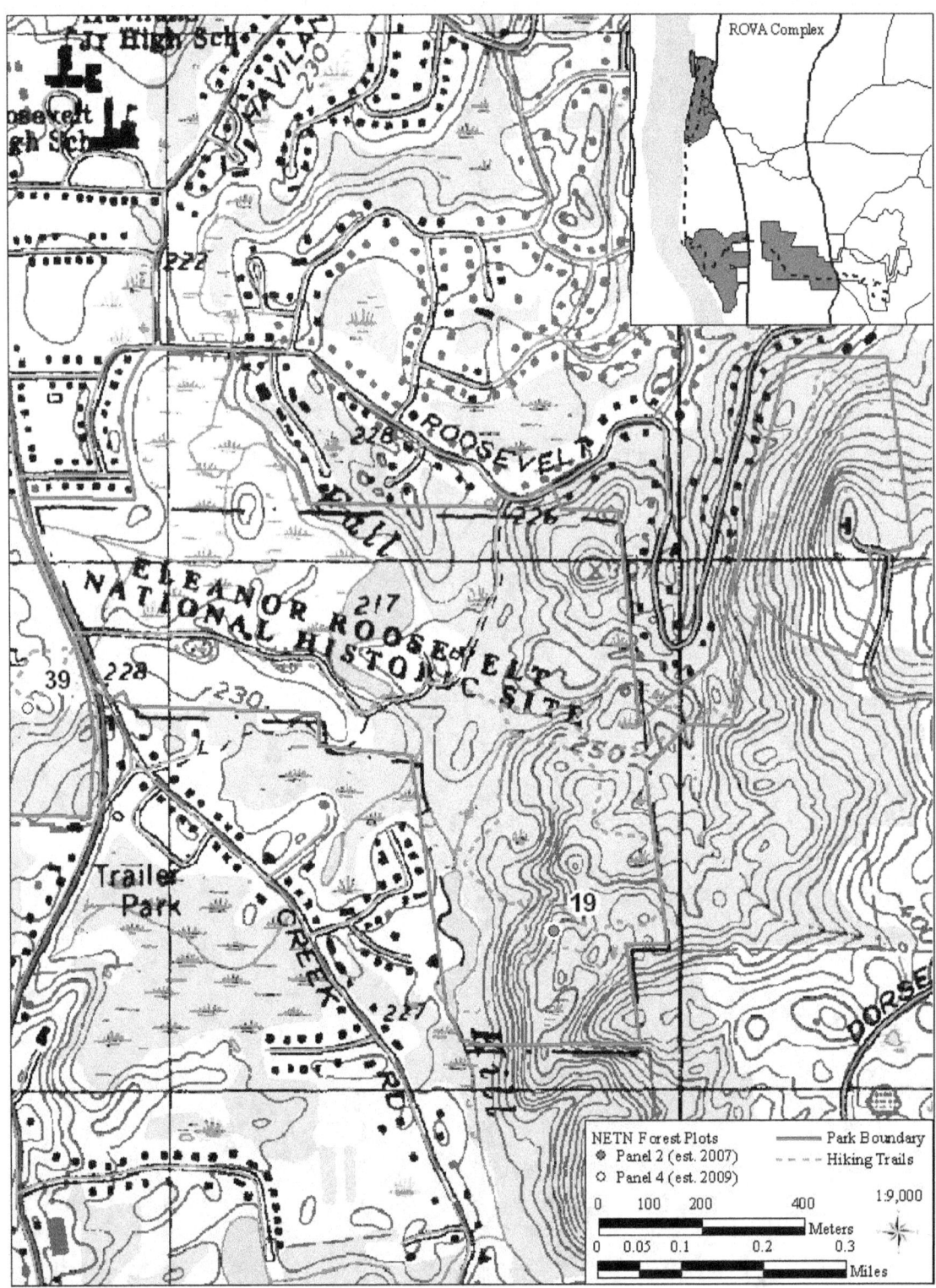

Figure B-2. Forest plot locations in Eleanor Roosevelt National Historic Site.

Appendix B. Forest plot locations in ACAD, MORR, ROVA and WEFA (continued)

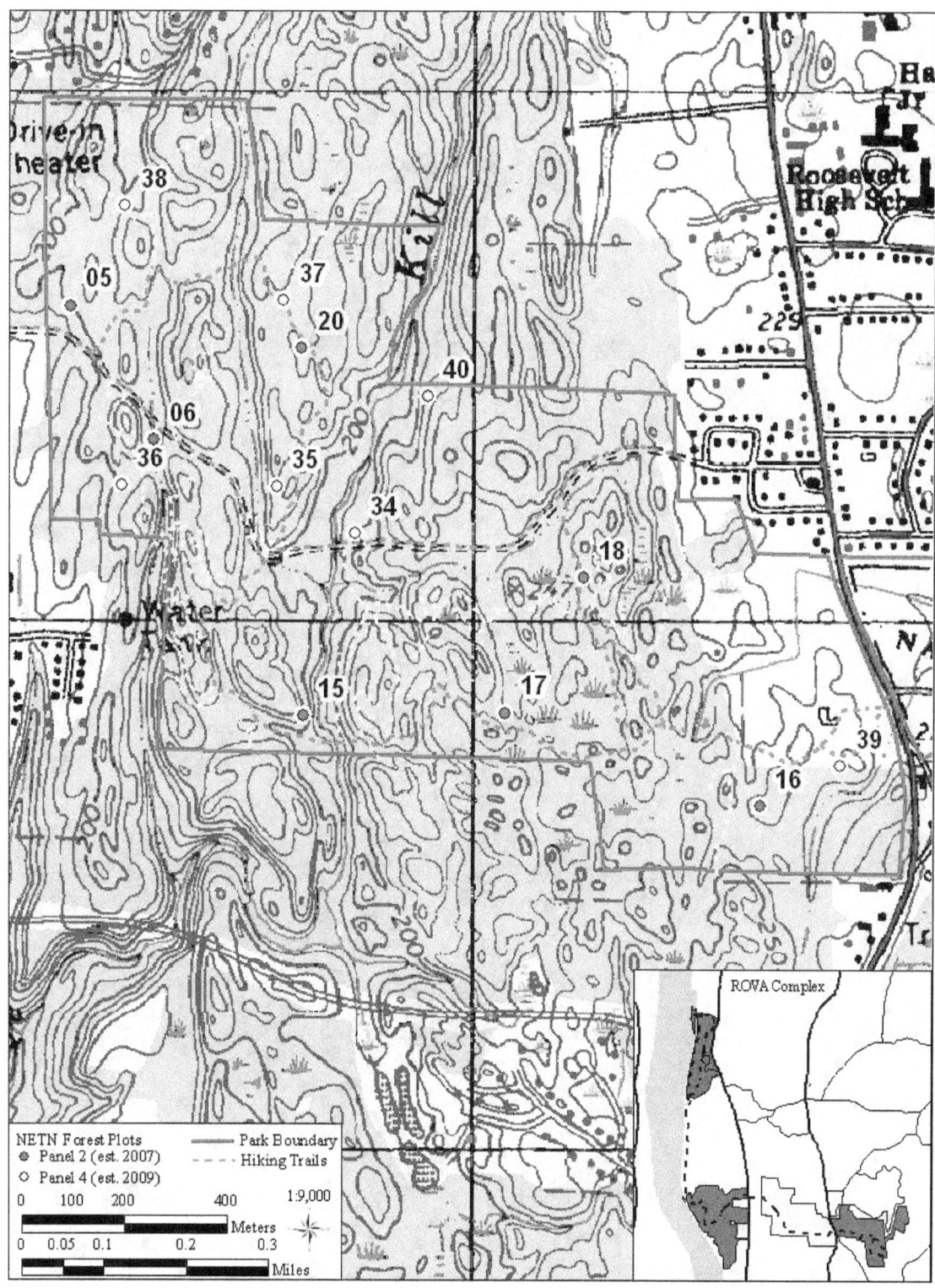

Figure B-3. Forest plot locations in the eastern section of Home of F.D.R. National Historic Site.

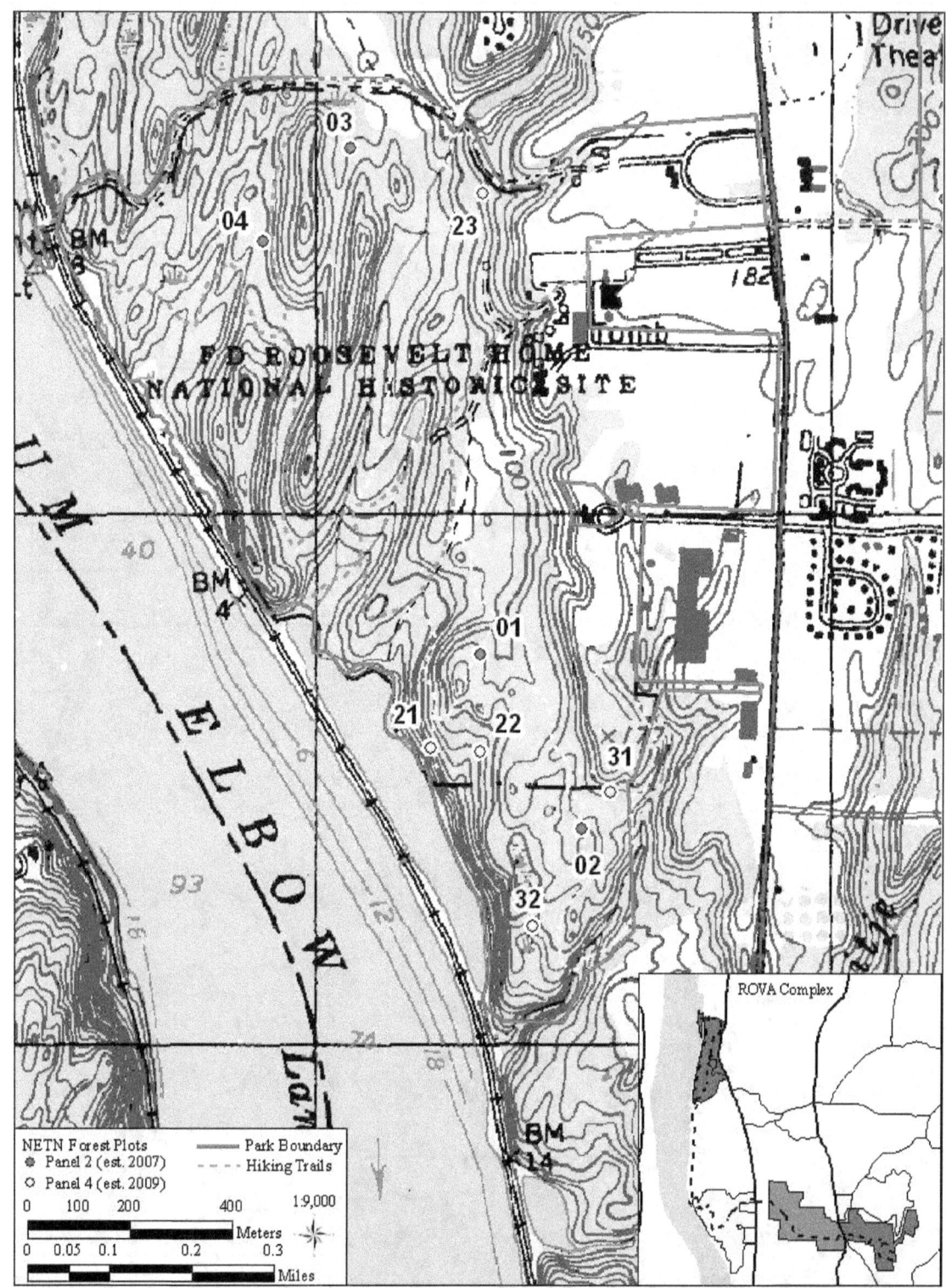

Figure B-4. Forest plot locations in the western section of Home of F.D.R. National Historic Site.

Appendix B. Forest plot locations in ACAD, MORR, ROVA and WEFA (continued)

Figure B-5. Forest plot locations in Morristown National Historical Park.

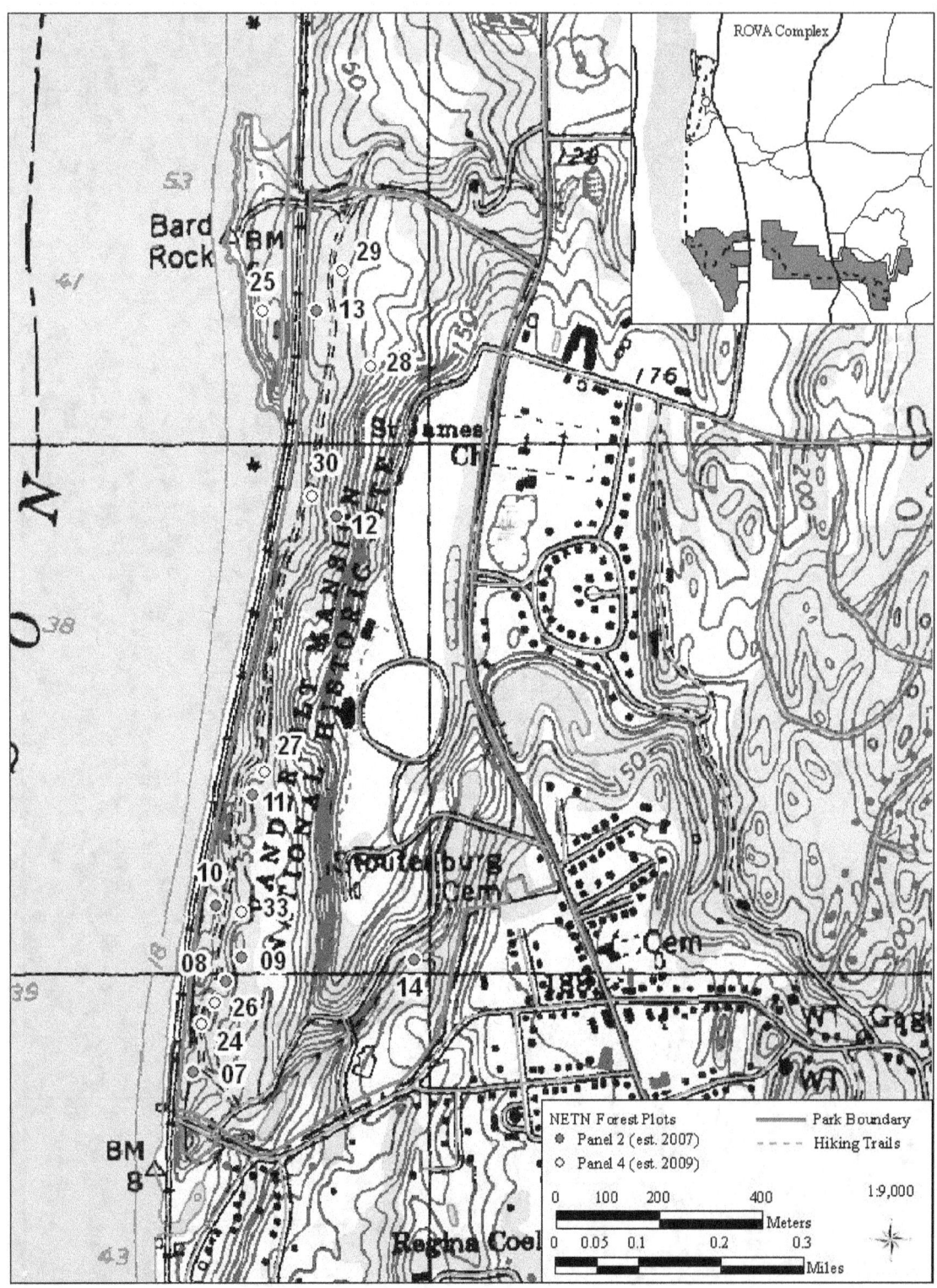

Figure B-6. Forest plot locations in Vanderbilt Mansion National Historic Site.

Appendix B. Forest plot locations in ACAD, MORR, ROVA and WEFA (continued)

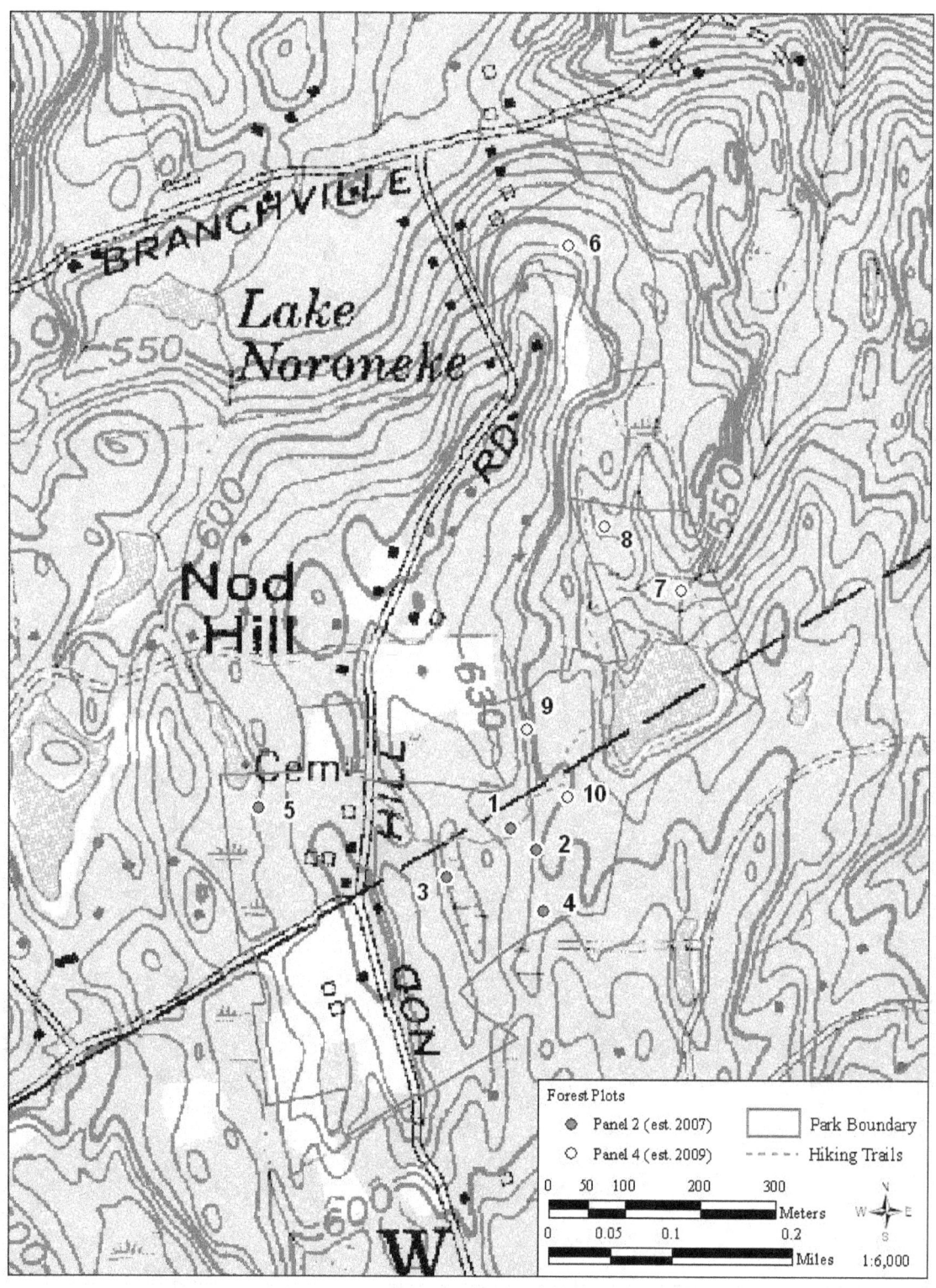

Figure B-7. Forest plot locations in Weir Farm National Historic Site.

Appendix C. Protocol implementation for the 2009 field season

Sampling Inconsistencies and Data Issues

Overall data quality for the 2009 field season was quite good. The 2009 dataset had less missing information and fewer errors than previous years. The addition of field checks, which required crew members to record their initials on each datasheet after they verified it was correct and complete, was likely an important factor in this improvement.

Several protocol deviations occurred early in the season while the crews were sampling plots in MORR. The first two inconsistencies concerned microplot sampling. One crew incorrectly defined an individual shrub as a clump of stems emerging from the same area even if they were not attached above ground. Each stem that was unattached above ground should have been counted, and the shrub tallies on these plots are off by roughly a factor of 10. Woody vine species were also mistakenly over-looked in the shrub tally by this crew, and common vine species (e.g., Japanese honeysuckle [*Lonicera japonica*] and poison ivy [*Toxicodendron radicans*]) were not tallied in several microplots. The last deviation from the protocol at a few MORR plots involved one crew incorrectly including consolidated leaf litter in the litter depth measurement. Leaf litter depth should only include unconsolidated litter, and the depth in these plots is 2-3 times more than it should be.

A recurring issue throughout the field season involved one team incorrectly recording a stand disturbance for only minor foliage herbivory. Where noticed during the data entry process, these records were removed. The forest protocol was revised to clarify that minor herbivory should not be considered a disturbance.

The biggest issue with data quality in 2009 was poor documentation of unknown species that were collected in or near the plot for later identification. This was especially the case in ACAD, and there are several outstanding specimens that were not traceable back to a plot. To avoid this issue in the future, we are requiring crews to fill out and attach pre-printed labels to the unknown specimen bags.

Quality Control and Quality Assurance (QA/QC)

To verify data quality and quantify sampling error, we resample 5% (4 plots) of the forest plots that the crews sample every year. Plots are randomly selected for QA/QC, with two plots located in ACAD and two plots located in a randomly selected national historical park or national historic site. WEFA plots 7 and 10, and ACAD plots 131 and 149 were sampled for QA/QC in 2009.

The only major issues that arose from QA/QC in WEFA concerned the timed plot search for additional species. QA/QC found 16 more species during the timed search on plot 7, and six more species on plot 10 than the crew and contract botanist found. Considering this, it is likely that species diversity in WEFA plots 6-10 is higher than our data show. The quadrat data did correspond fairly well between the crew and QA/QC.

QA/QC results for ACAD revealed a few minor errors, but overall the crew and QA/QC data were close. Stand structure at plot 131 was incorrectly recorded as "multi-aged" forest by the crew, when it should have been recorded as "woodland." Plot 131 had a very dense shrub layer composed of multiple ericaceous shrubs which were hard to distinguish and tally correctly. As a result, rhodora (*Rhododendron canadense*) was mistakenly identified and tallied as sheep laurel (*Kalmia angustifolia*). Leatherleaf (*Chamaedaphne calyculata*) was missed on one microplot by the crew. On ACAD plot 149, the crew defined the codominant layer in the canopy differently than QA/QC. Also on plot 149, the crew tended to find more tree conditions, whereas QA/QC found more foliage conditions.

Protocol Revisions

The forest protocol undergoes an in-house review by NETN and Mid-Atlantic Network (MIDN) staff at the end of every field season. This review is where most decisions are made regarding changes to the protocol, and discussion topics typically include lessons learned during the field season, crew feedback, and potential protocol and database changes that came up during the field season. Based on the review, the following revisions were made to the protocol:

Shrub stem tallies in microplots have proven time-consuming and somewhat unrepeatable in plots with dense understories. Starting in 2010 we will quantify shrub abundance by estimating percent cover of each shrub species in microplots. Tree seedlings will continue to be sampled using stem tallies by size class.

We continue to look for ways to make the NETN and MIDN sampling procedures more similar. Starting in 2010, NETN will use a slightly modified version of MIDN tree status codes.

The original definition of a multiple intersection for coarse woody debris (CWD) was when one piece crossed the same transect multiple times. A piece that crossed two different transects was recorded twice without noting that it was the same piece, and was thus included in CWD metric calculations twice. Starting in 2010, we will track any piece that crosses the same or multiple transects more than once. We will continue to calculate CWD metrics as before, but tracking the number of times a piece is recorded will give us the option to adjust CWD metric calculations in the future.

The deer browse index that was adopted in 2009 from the Eastern Rivers and Mountains Network protocol did not work well in ACAD because many of the species used to determine the index are uncommon in the park for reasons other than deer browse. Starting in 2010 we will use an adapted deer browse index for ACAD that relies less on presence of browse-preferred or non-preferred species, and more on degree of deer evidence (e.g., deer trails, scat, and browse) in the plot.

One final protocol change was made mid-season in 2009 after we discovered a forest plot in ACAD that had been vandalized. Most of the stakes and nearly all of the tree tags were removed making it impossible to determine the exact location of plot center. In 2010 we will reestablish this plot based on our best estimate of where plot center was located. If this plot is vandalized again, we will reestablish it with rebar and possibly scribe trees in the plot. While we hope this was an isolated event, we began mapping trees relative to plot center and marking witness trees with a white paint square. These data will allow us to reestablish a plot fairly accurately as long as the witness trees are identifiable. All of the plots established in ACAD in 2009 have been mapped. All other plots will be mapped the next time they are sampled.

Appendix D. Key invasive exotic plant indicator species of forest, woodland and successional ecosystems in the northeastern U.S. that were used in the NETN Ecological Integrity Scorecard.

Latin name	Common name	Habitat
Acer platanoides	Norway maple	Open & forest habitats
Ailanthus altissima	Tree-of-heaven	Edges & successional habitats
Alliaria petiolata	Garlic mustard	Open & forest habitats
Berberis thunbergii	Japanese barberry	Open & forest habitats
Berberis vulgaris	European barberry	Open & wooded habitats
Cardamine impatiens	Narrowleaf bittercress	Open & wooded habitats
Celastrus orbiculatus	Oriental bittersweet	Edges & successional habitats
Cynanchum louiseae	Black swallow-wort	Open, successional & wooded habitats
Cynanchum rossicum	European swallow-wort	Open, successional & wooded habitats
Euonymus alata	Winged burning bush	Open, successional & wooded habitats
Frangula alnus	Glossy buckthorn	Wetland & successional habitats
Ligustrum spp. *(obtusifolium, vulgare)*	Privet	Successional & forest habitats
Lonicera japonica	Japanese honeysuckle	Edges & successional habitats
Lonicera spp. *(morrowii, tatarica, x bella)*	Exotic honeysuckles	Open & successional habitats
Luzula luzuloides	Forest woodrush	Open & wooded habitats
Microstegium vimineum	Japanese stiltgrass	Open & forest habitats
Polygonum caespitosum	Oriental ladysthumb	Open & successional habitats
Polygonum cuspidatum	Japanese knotweed	Riparian, open & successional habitats
Rhamnus cathartica	Common buckthorn	Riparian, open & successional habitats
Rhodotypos scandens	jetbead	Open, successional & wooded habitats
Rosa multiflora	Multiflora rose	Open & successional habitats
Rubus phoenicolasius	Wineberry	Open, successional & wooded habitats

Appendix E. Diameter distribution and species composition graphs

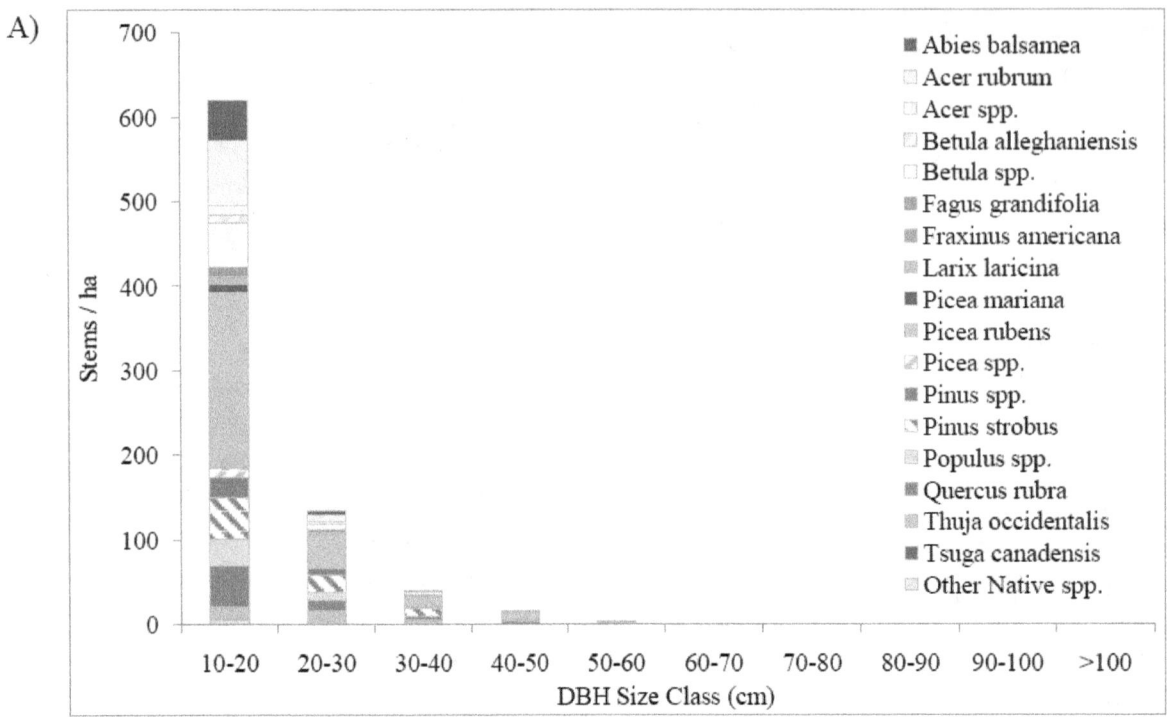

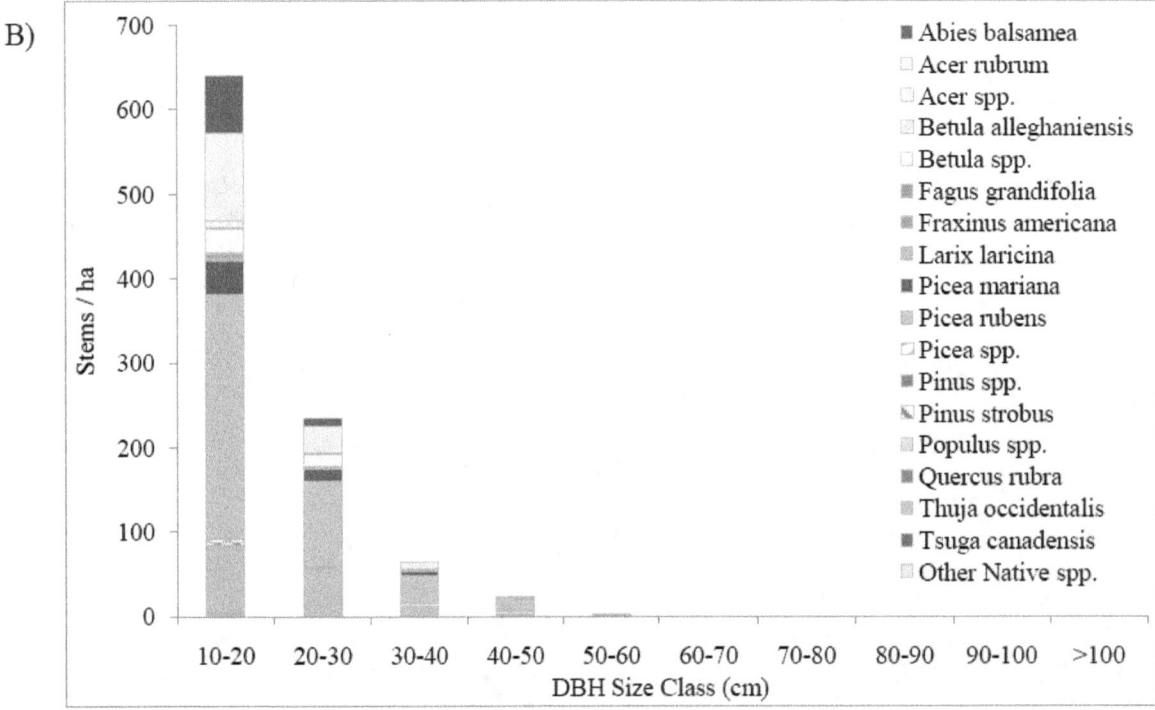

Figure E-1. Tree diameter distribution of forest plots in Acadia National Park subunits A) eastern Mount Desert Island (n = 79), and B) western Mount Desert Island (n = 62).

Appendix E. Diameter distribution and species composition graphs (continued)

A)

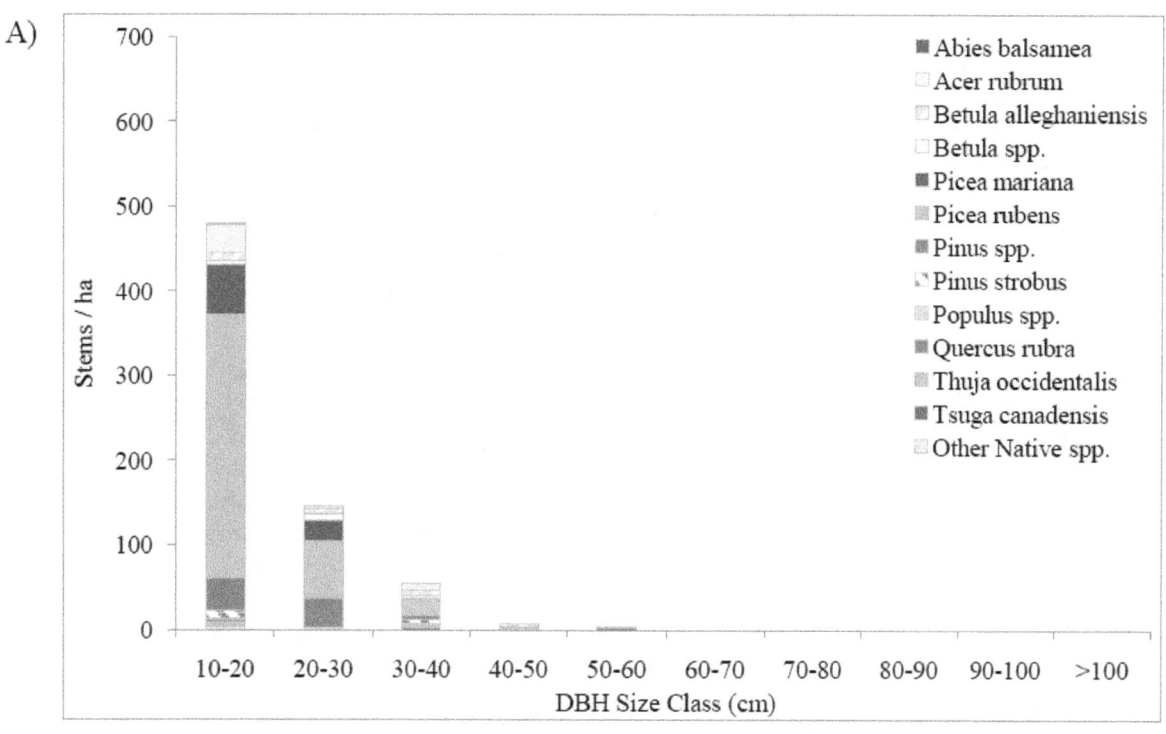

B)

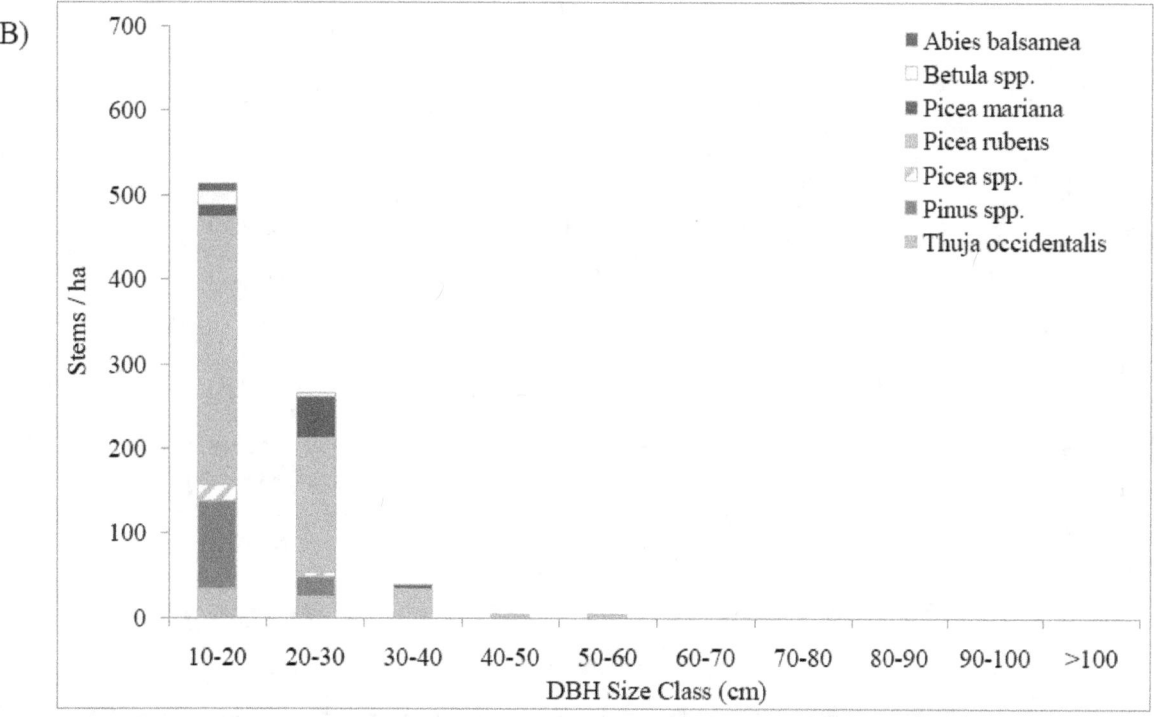

Figure E-2. Tree diameter distribution of forest plots in Acadia National Park subunits A) Isle au Haut (n = 19) and B) Schoodic Peninsula (n = 9).

Appendix E. Diameter distribution and species composition graphs (continued)

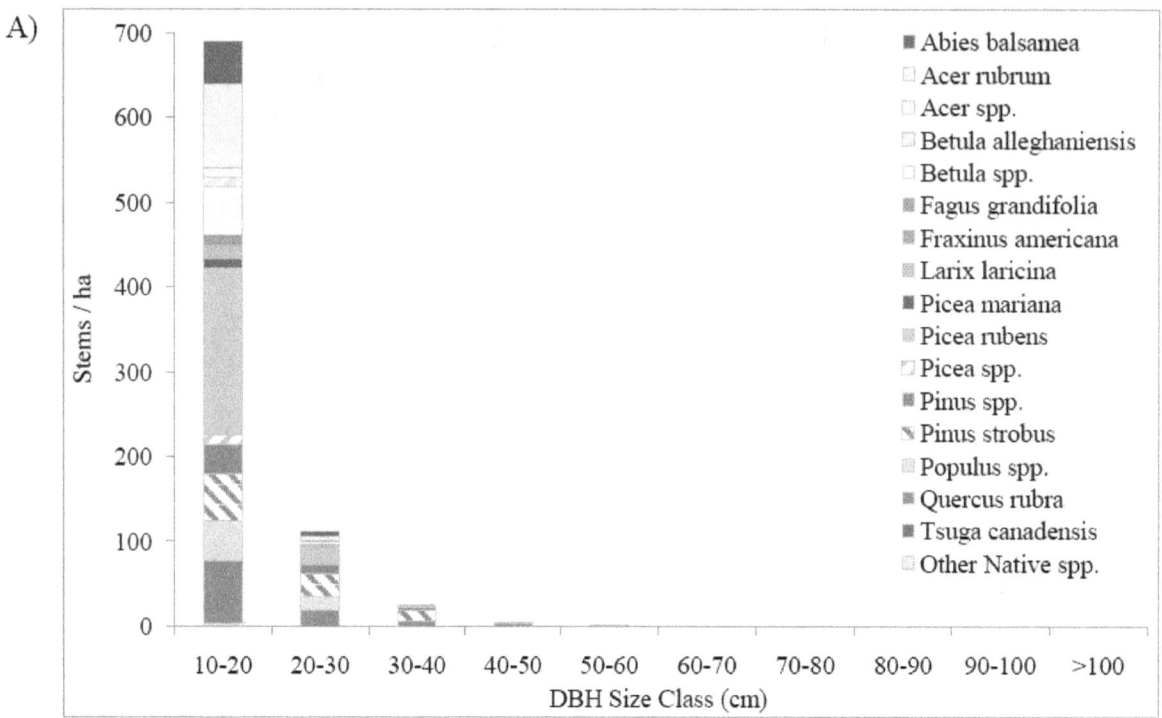

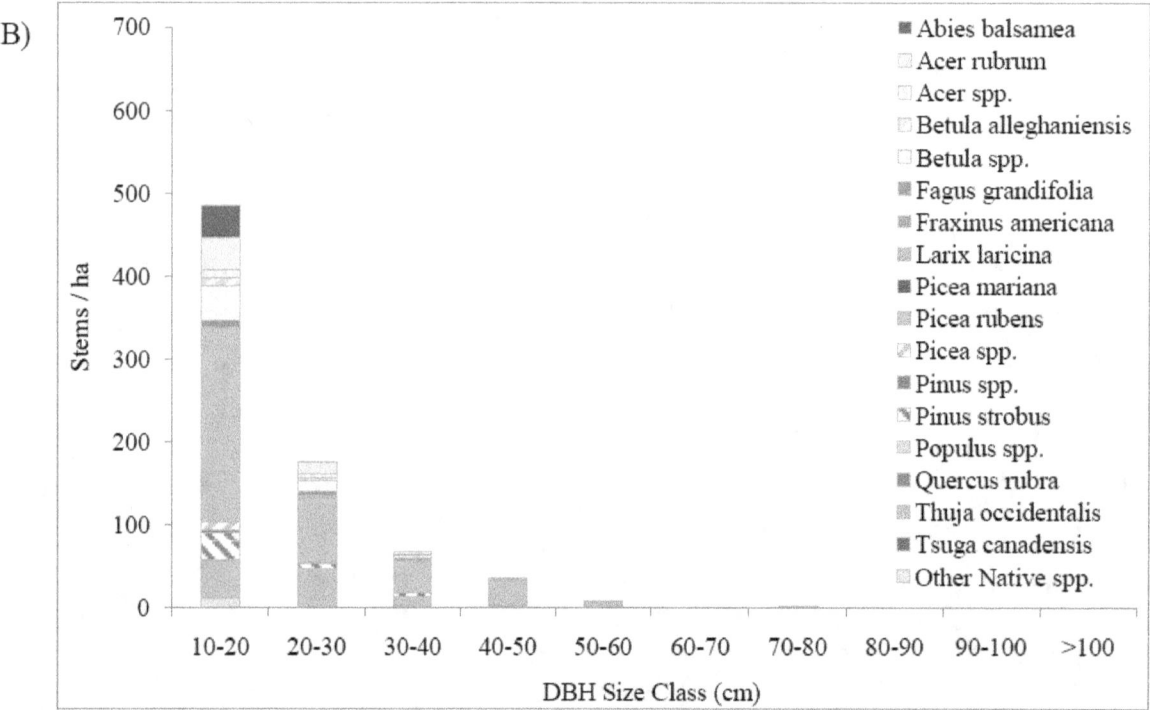

Figure E-3. Acadia National Park tree diameter distribution on Eastern Mount Desert Island in A) forest plots within the boundary of the 1947 fire (n = 52), and B) plots that were not within the 1947 fire boundary (n = 27).

Appendix E. Diameter distribution and species composition graphs (continued)

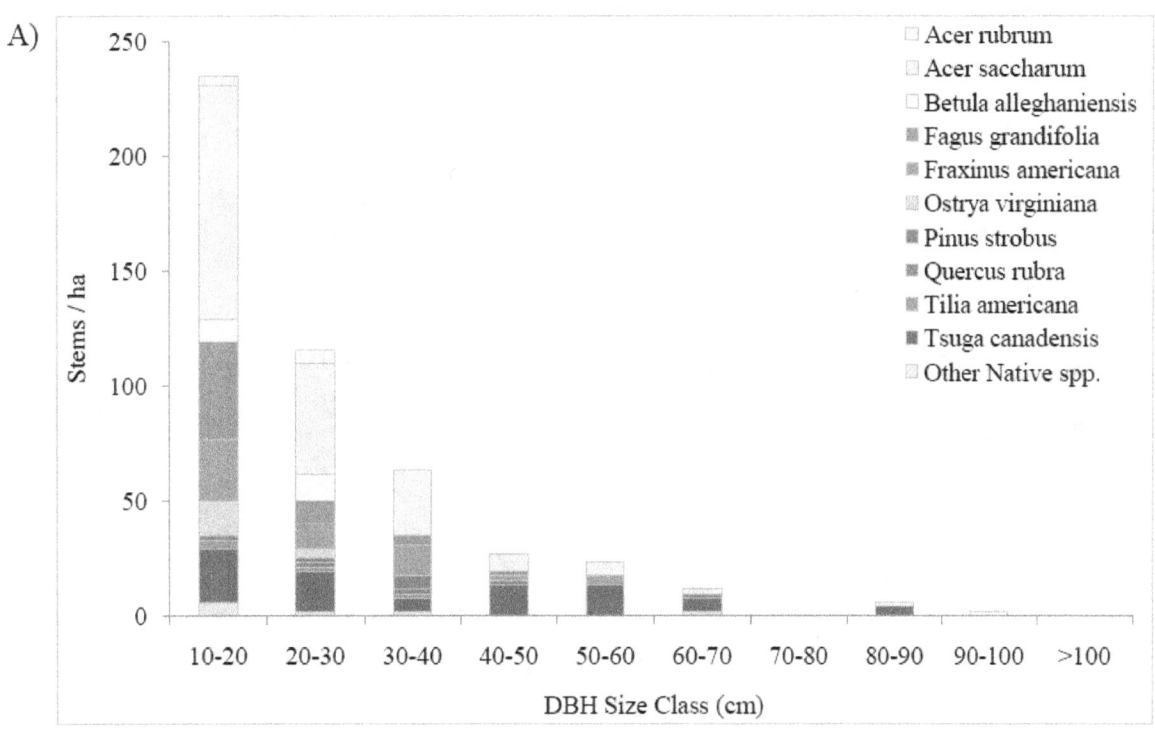

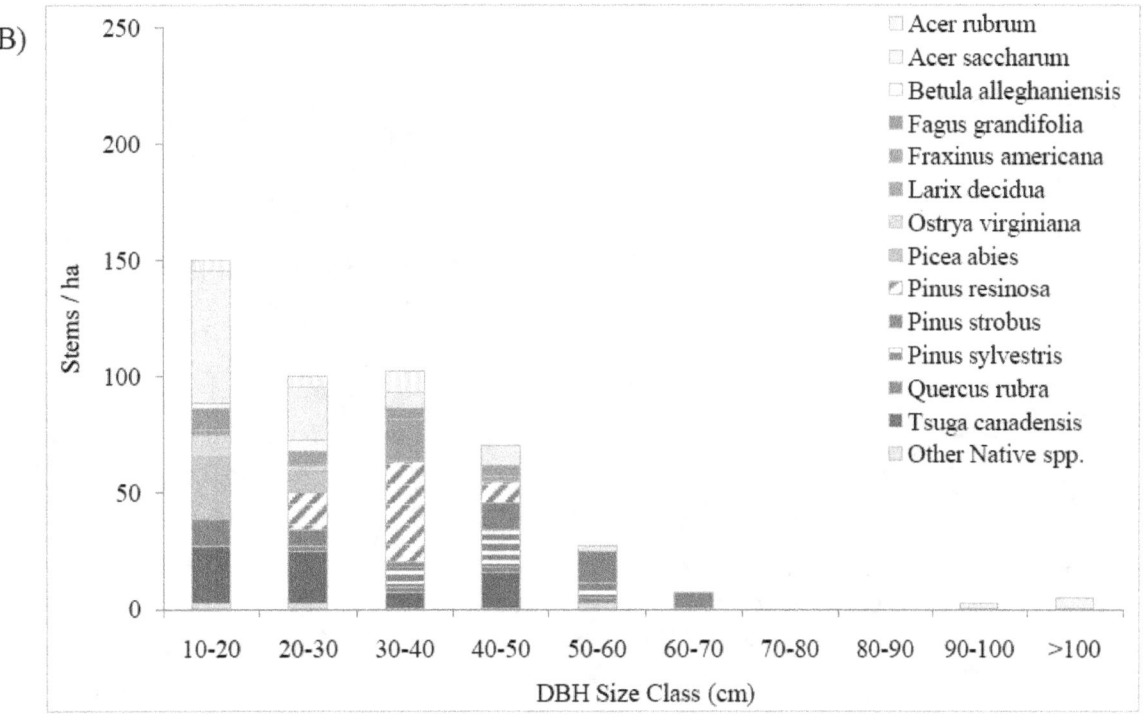

Figure E-4. Marsh-Billings-Rockefeller NHP tree diameter distribution of forest plots in A) natural forest (n = 13) and B) forest plantations (n = 11).

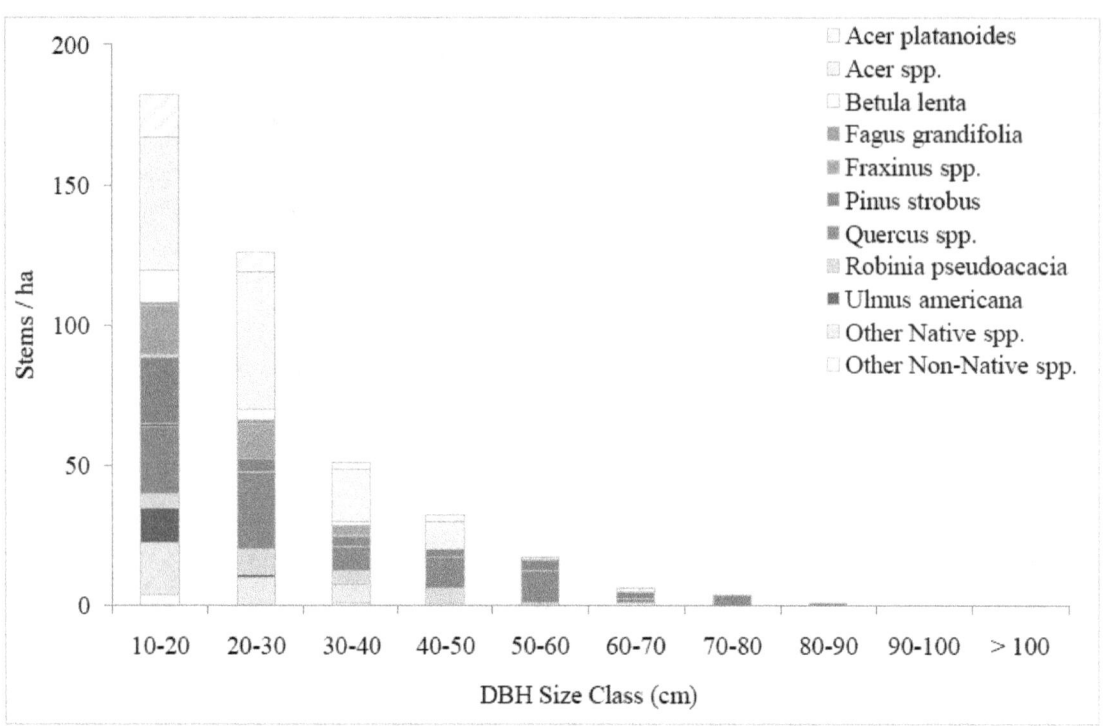

Figure E-5. Minute Man NHP tree diameter distribution of forest plots (n = 20).

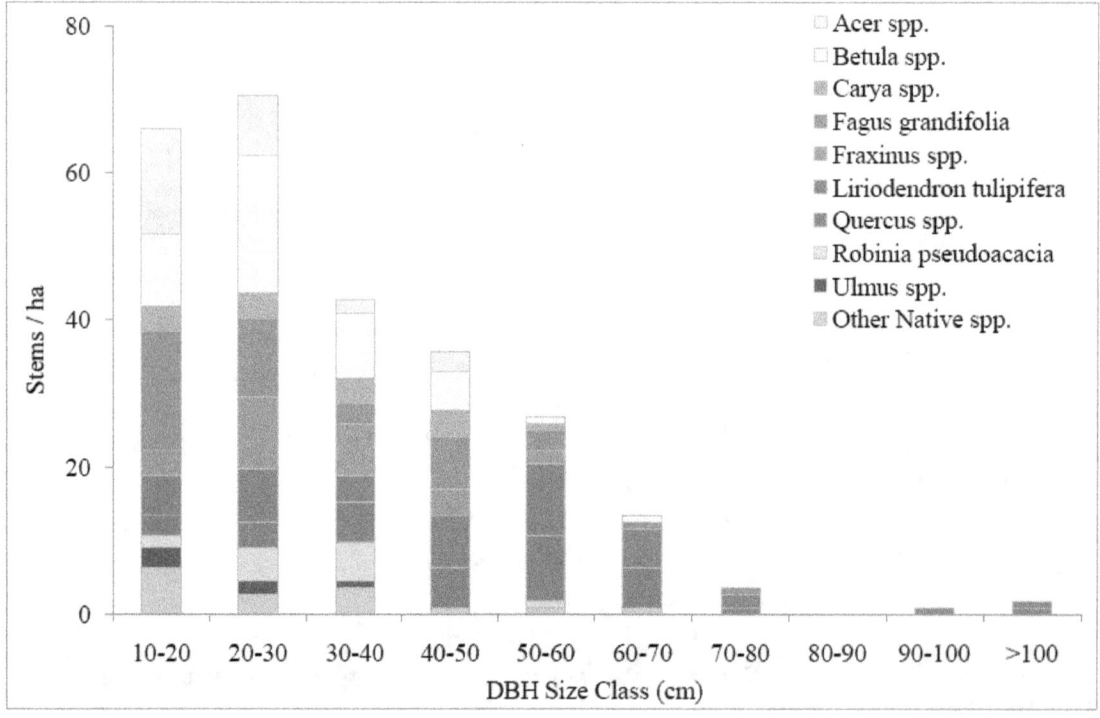

Figure E-6. Morristown NHP tree diameter distribution of forest plots (n = 28).

Appendix E. Diameter distribution and species composition graphs (continued)

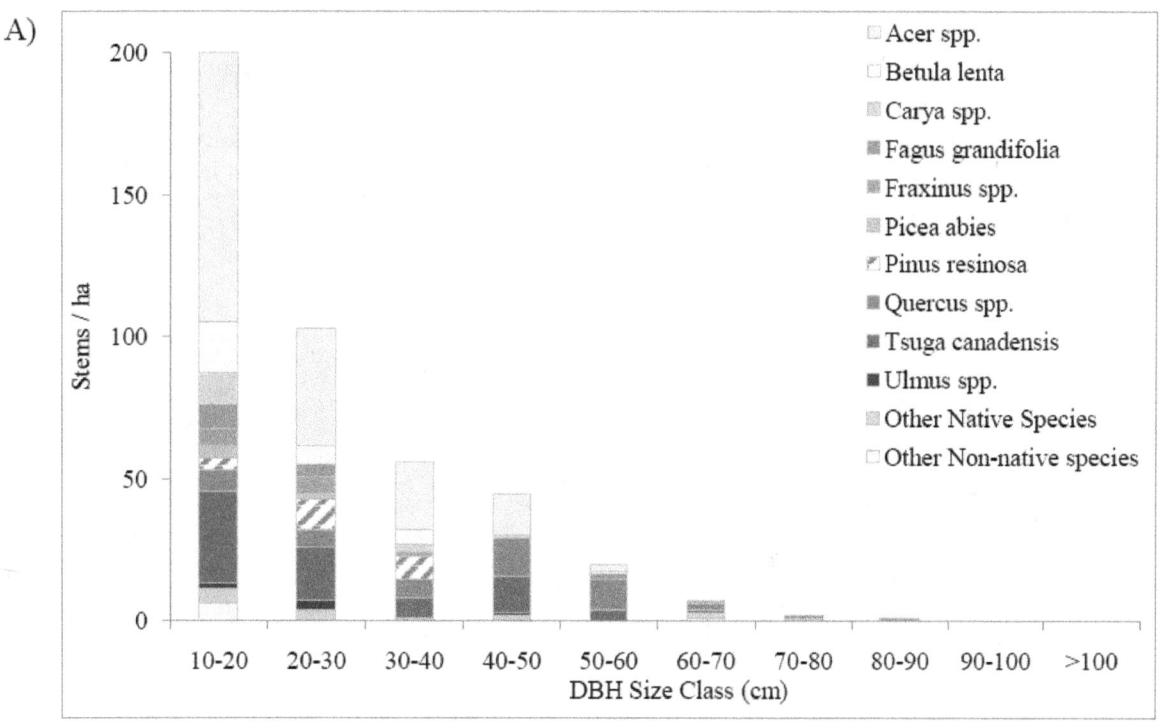

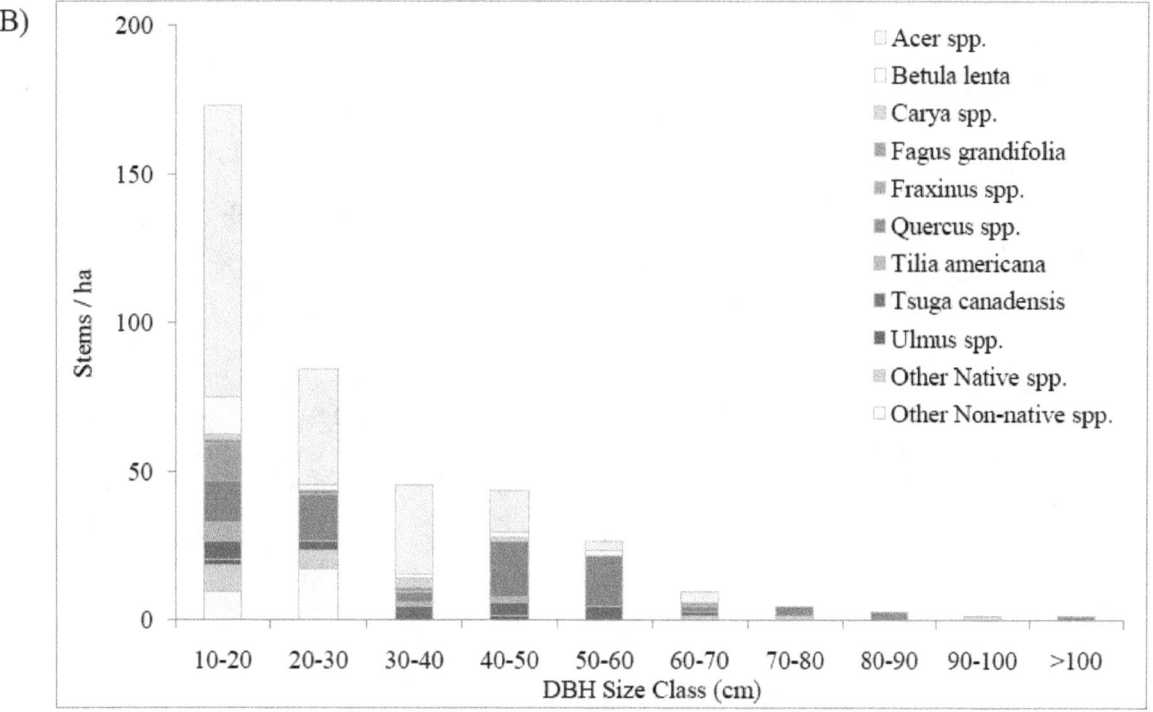

Figure E-7. Roosevelt-Vanderbilt NHS tree diameter distribution of forest plots in A) Eleanor Roosevelt NHS and Home of FDR NHS (n = 24) and B) Vanderbilt Mansion NHS (n = 16).

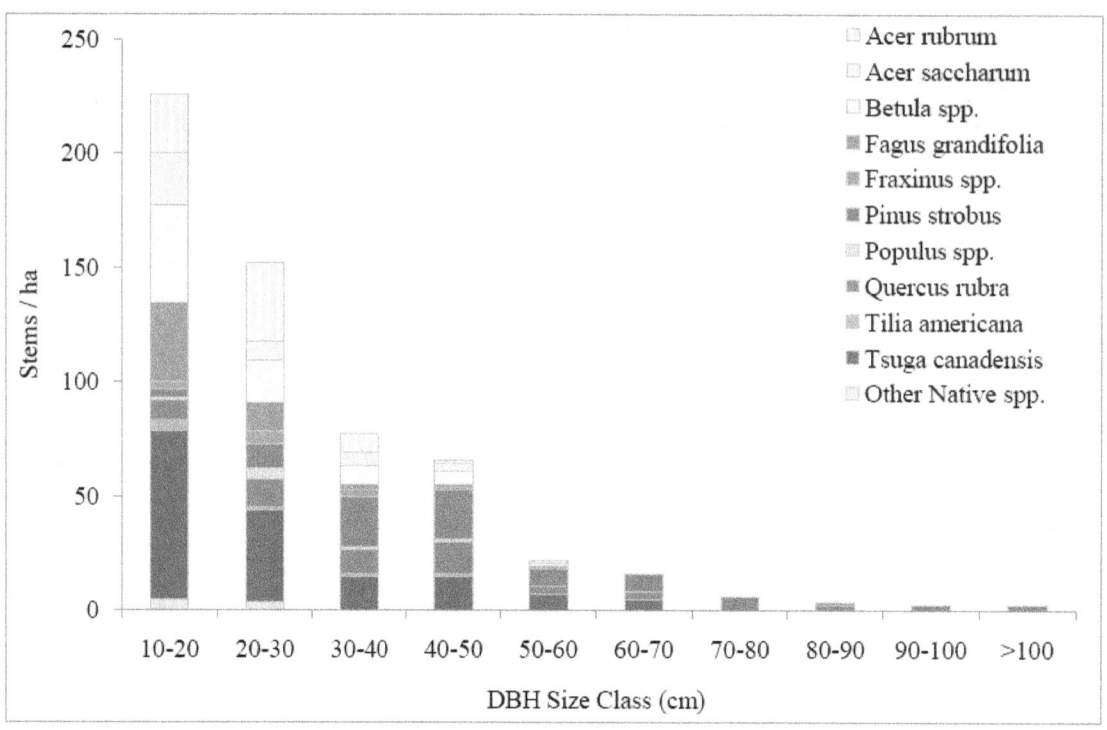

Figure E-8. Saint-Gaudens NHS tree diameter distribution of forest plots (n = 21).

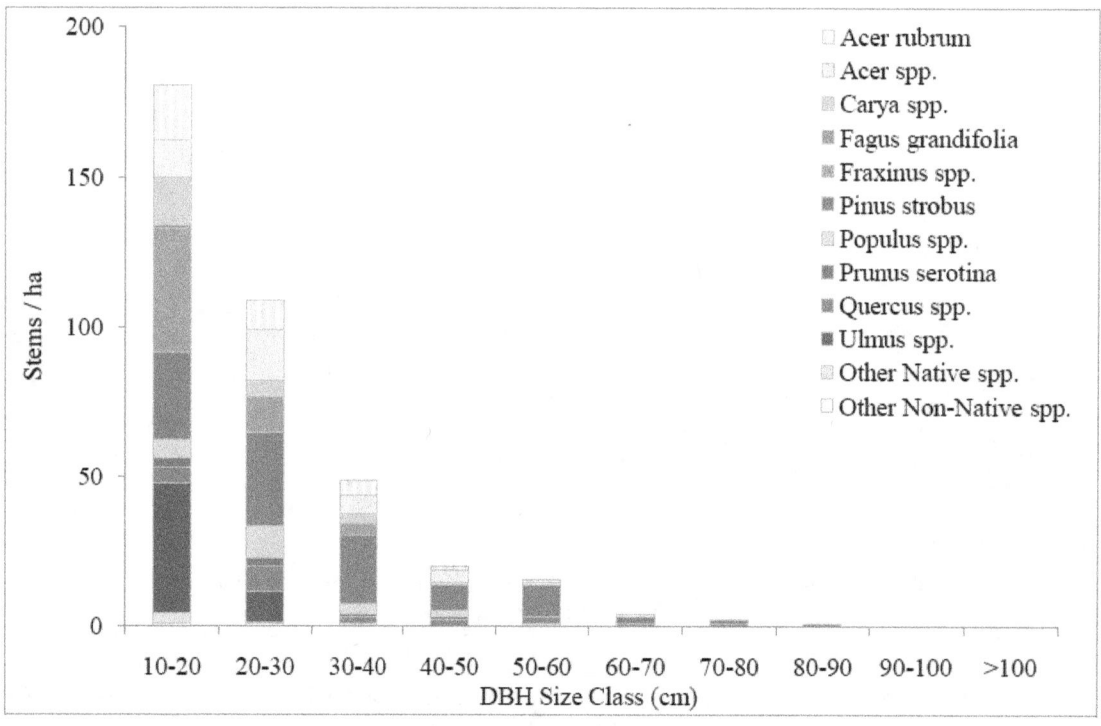

Figure E-9. Saratoga NHP tree diameter distribution of forest plots (n = 32).

Appendix E. Diameter distribution and species composition graphs (continued)

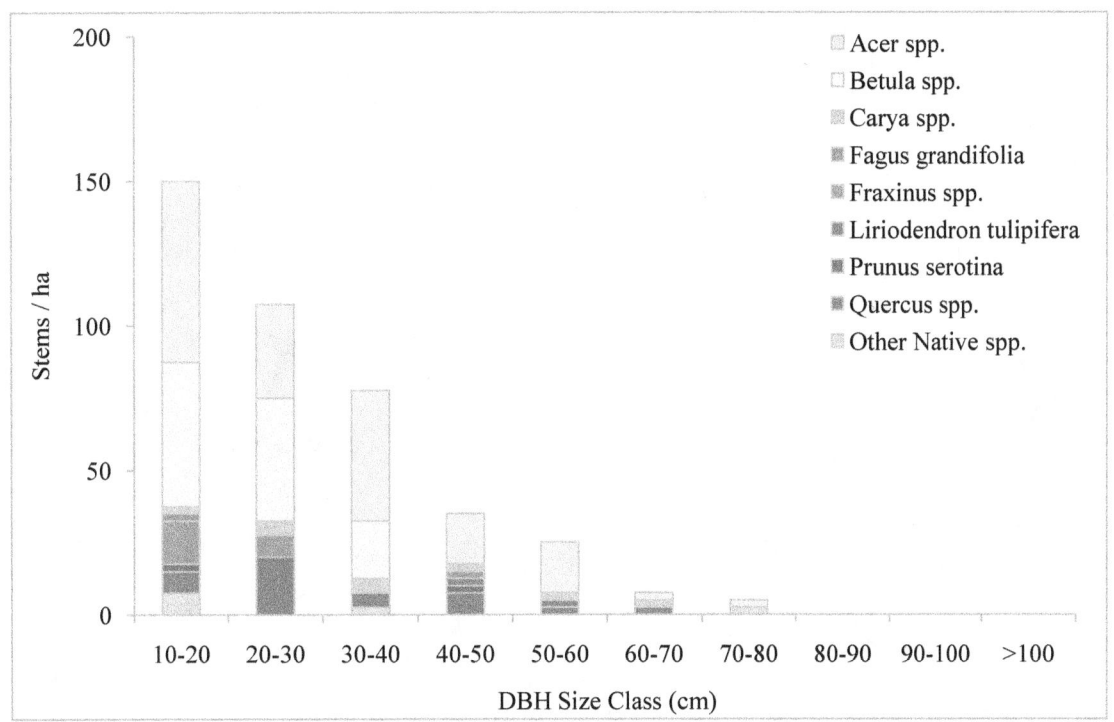

Figure E-10. Weir Farm NHS tree diameter distribution of forest plots (n = 10).

Appendix F. Seedling and sapling density graphs

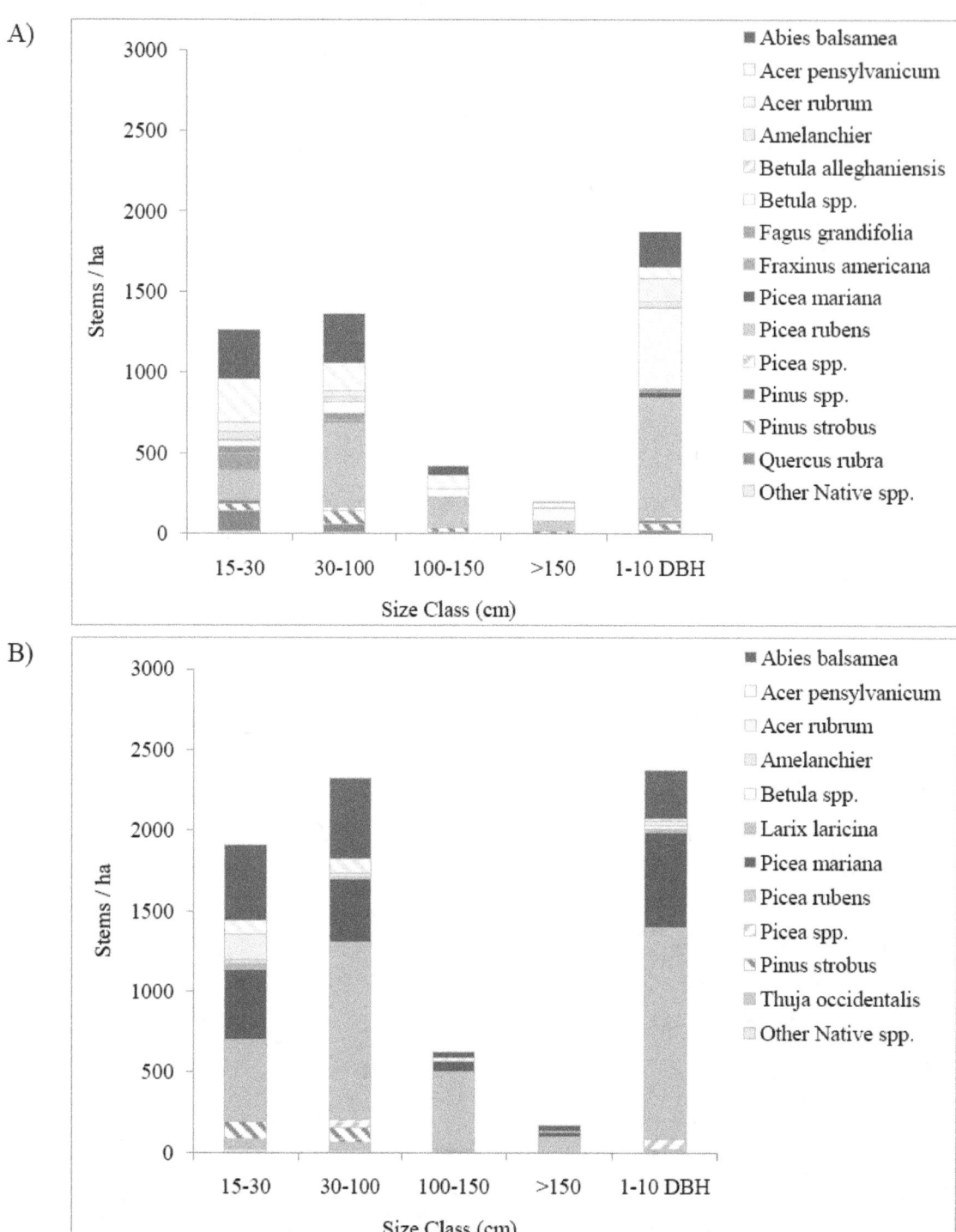

Figure F-1. Density of seedlings and saplings in Acadia National Park in A) eastern Mount Desert Island (n = 79) and B) western Mount Desert Island (n = 62). Classes 15-30, 30-100, 100-150 and > 150 cm (for individuals with diameter at breast height < 1) reflect seedling height, and 1-10 DBH reflects sapling diameter at breast height.

54

Appendix F. Seedling and sapling density graphs (continued)

A)

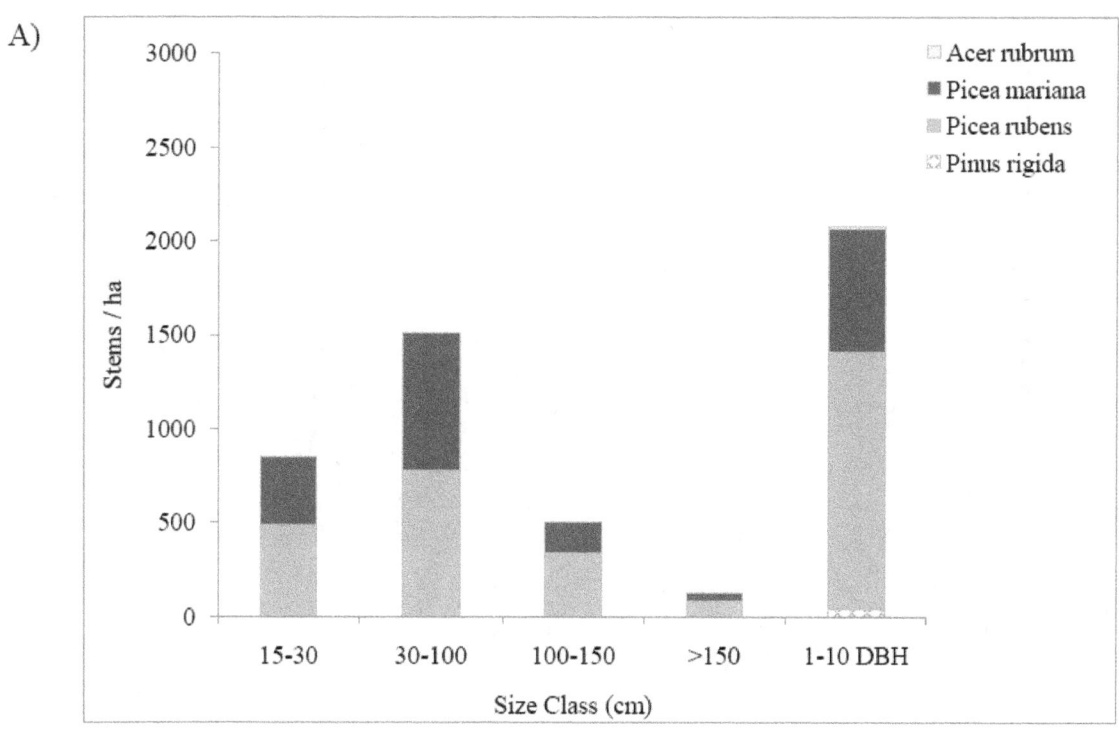

B)

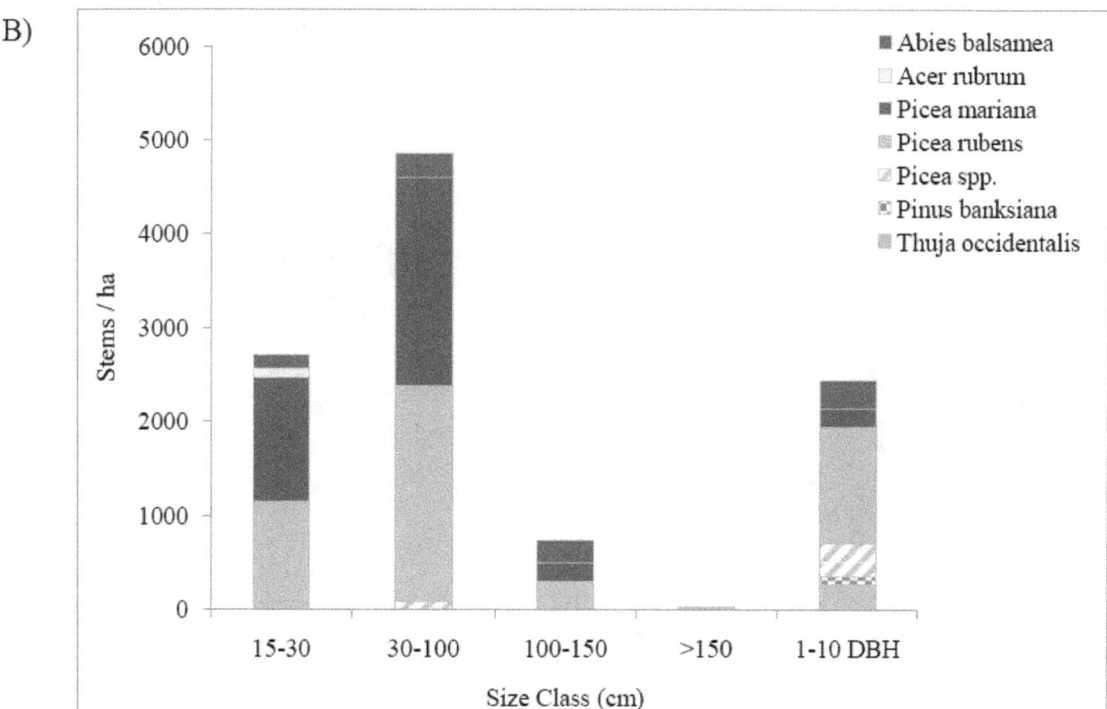

Figure F-2. Density of seedlings and saplings in Acadia National Park in A) Isle au Haut (n = 19) and B) Schoodic peninsula (n = 9). Classes 15-30, 30-100, 100-150 and > 150 cm (for individuals with diameter at breast height < 1 cm) reflect seedling height, and 1-10 DBH reflects sapling diameter at breast height.

Appendix F. Seedling and sapling density graphs (continued)

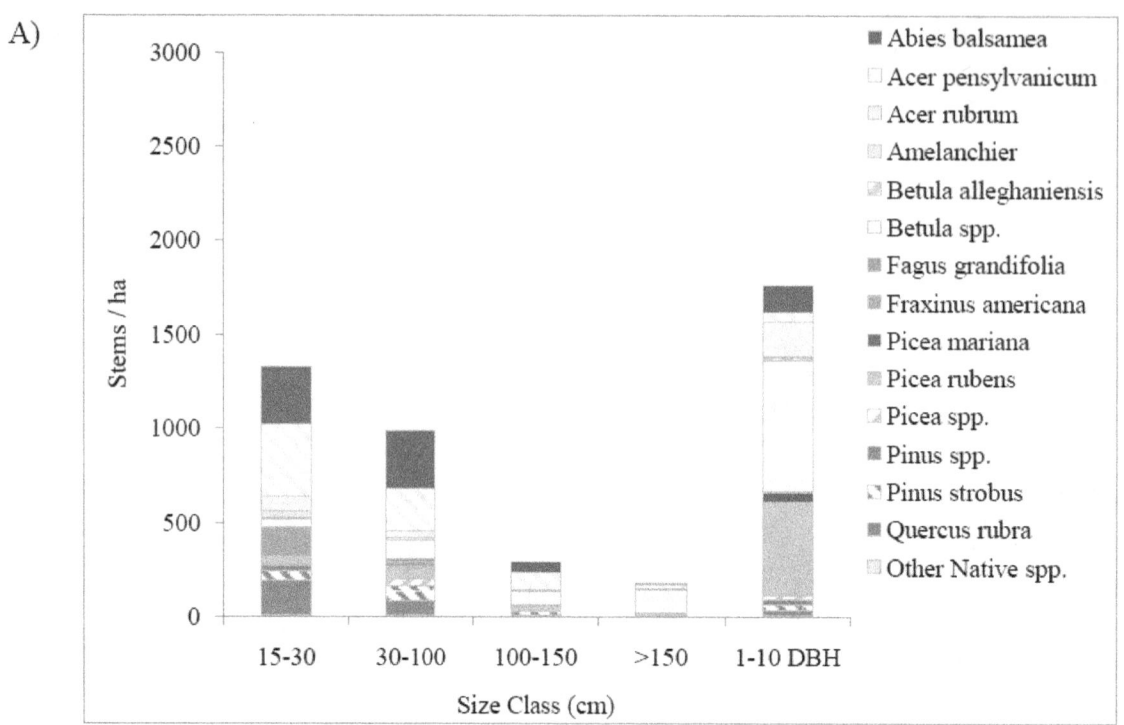

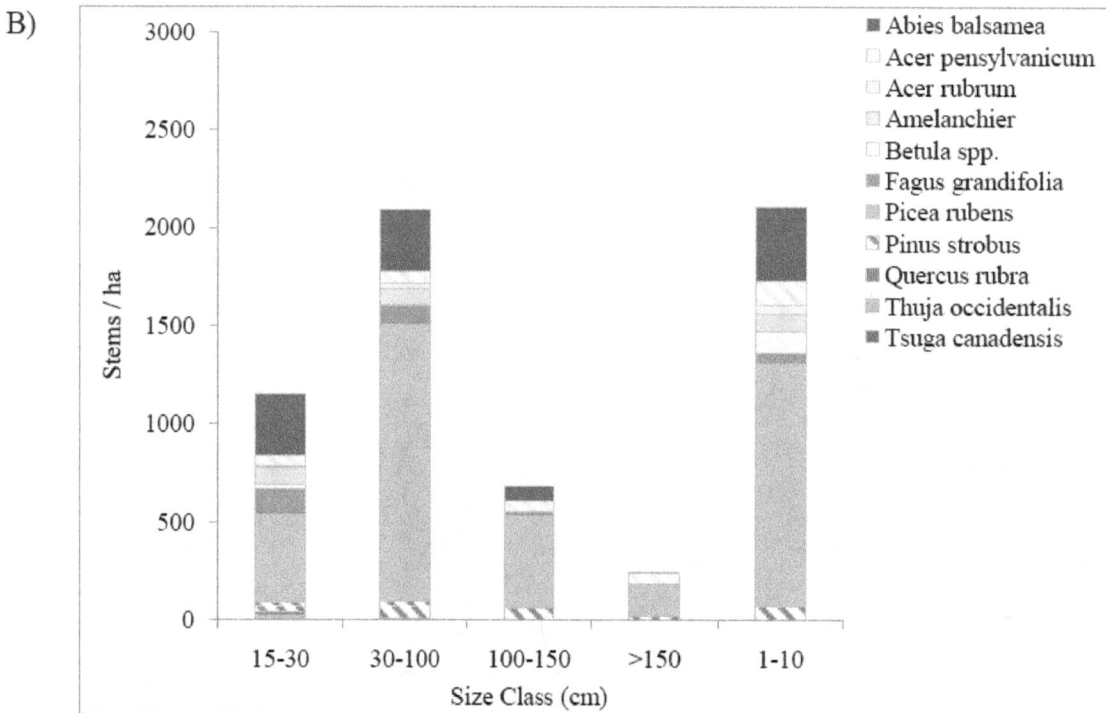

Figure F-3. Density of seedlings and saplings in Acadia National Park on Eastern Mount Desert Island in A) forest plots within the boundary of the 1947 fire (n = 52) and B) forest plots that were not within the 1947 fire boundary (n = 27). Classes 15-30, 30-100, 100-150 and >150 cm (for individuals with diameter at breast height < 1) reflect seedling height, and 1-10 DBH reflects sapling diameter at breast height.

Appendix F. Seedling and sapling density graphs (continued)

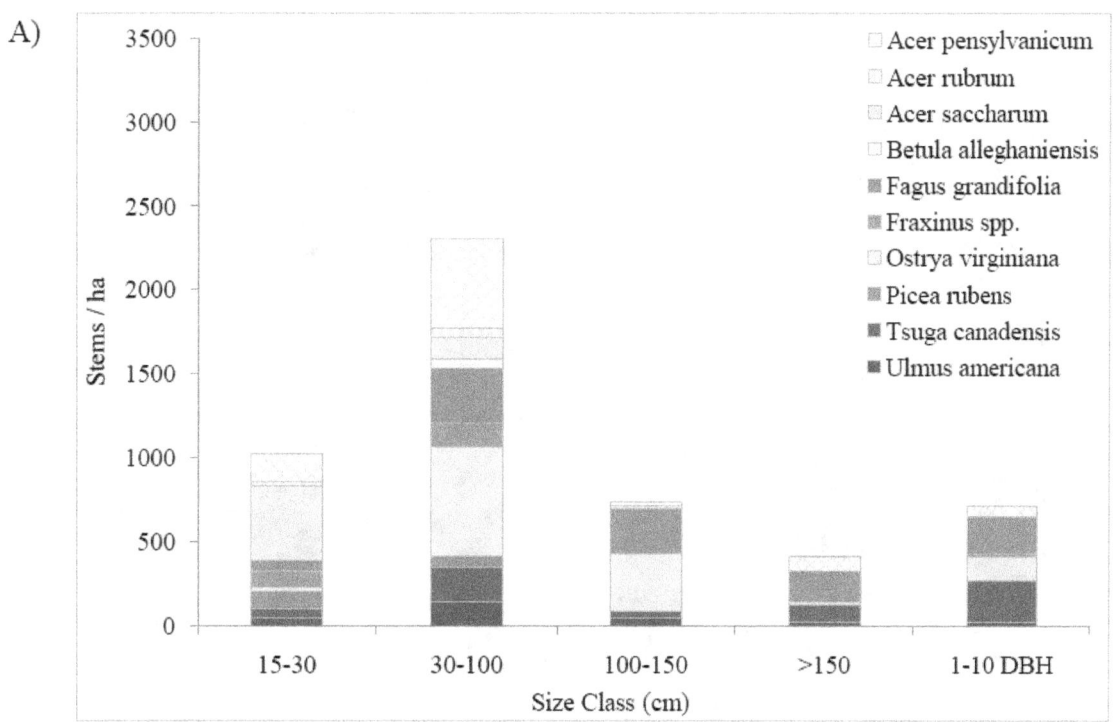

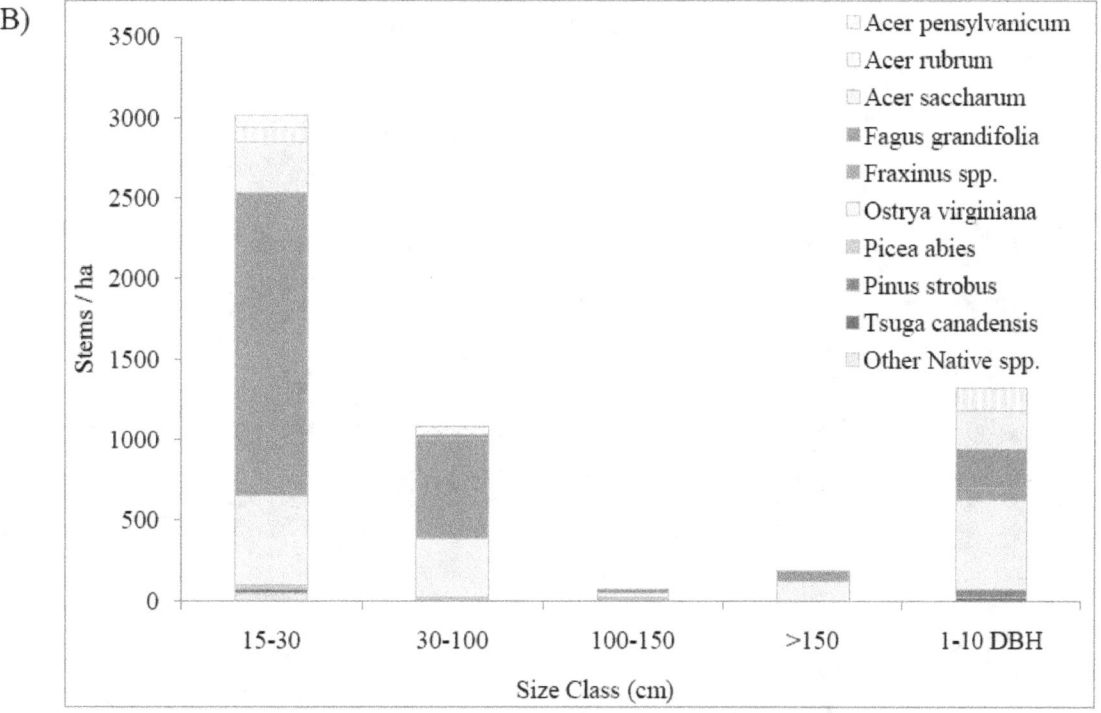

Figure F-4. Density of seedlings and saplings in Marsh-Billings-Rockefeller NHP in A) natural forest and B) forest plantations. Classes 15-30, 30-100, 100-150 and > 150cm (for individuals with diameter at breast height < 1) reflect seedling height, and 1-10 DBH reflects sapling diameter at breast height.

Appendix F. Seedling and sapling density graphs (continued)

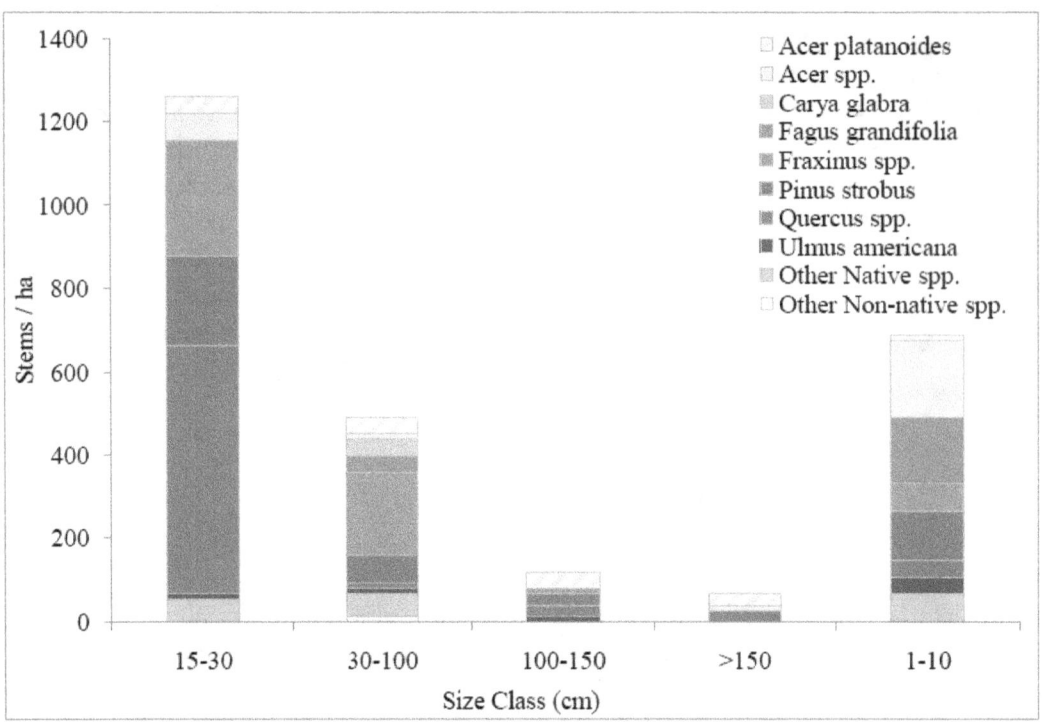

Figure F-5. Density of seedlings and saplings in Minute Man NHP. Classes 15-30, 30-100, 100-150 and > 150cm (for individuals with diameter at breast height < 1) reflect seedling height, and 1-10 DBH reflects sapling diameter at breast height.

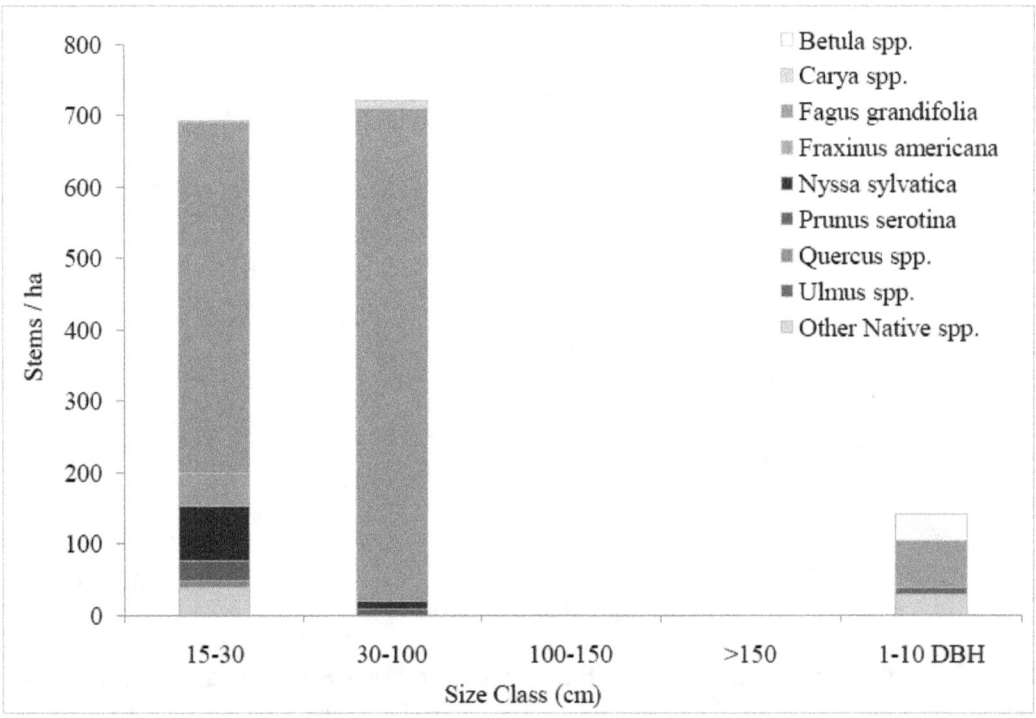

Figure F-6. Density of seedlings and saplings in Morristown NHP. Classes 15-30, 30-100, 100-150 and >150cm (for individuals with diameter at breast height < 1) reflect seedling height, and 1-10 DBH reflects sapling diameter at breast height.

Appendix F. Seedling and sapling density graphs (continued)

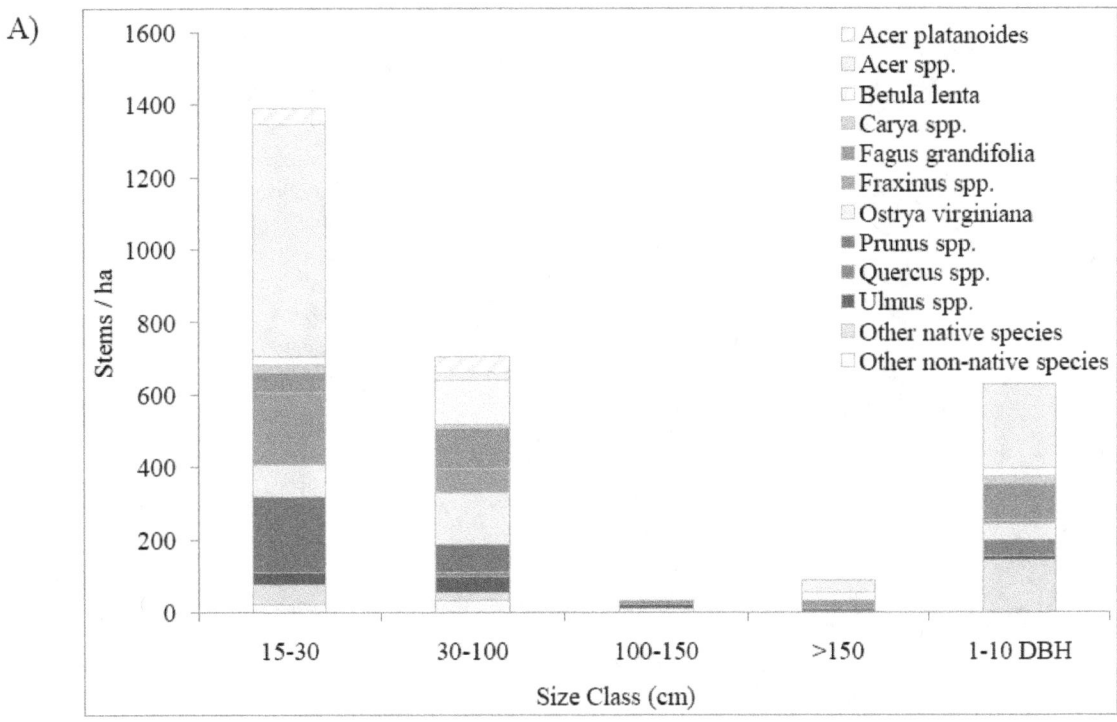

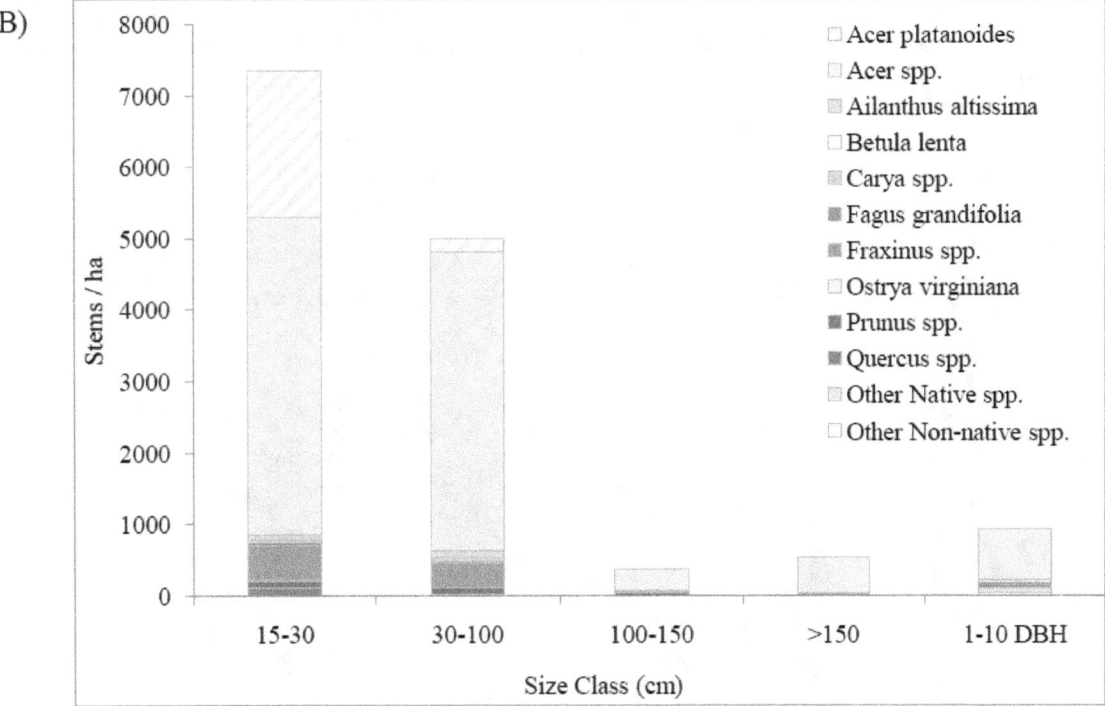

Figure F-7. Density of seedlings and saplings in Roosevelt-Vanderbilt NHS in A) Eleanor Roosevelt NHS and Home of FDR NHS and B) Vanderbilt Mansion NHS. Classes 15-30, 30-100, 100-150 and > 150cm (for individuals with diameter at breast height < 1) reflect seedling height, and 1-10 DBH reflects sapling diameter at breast height.

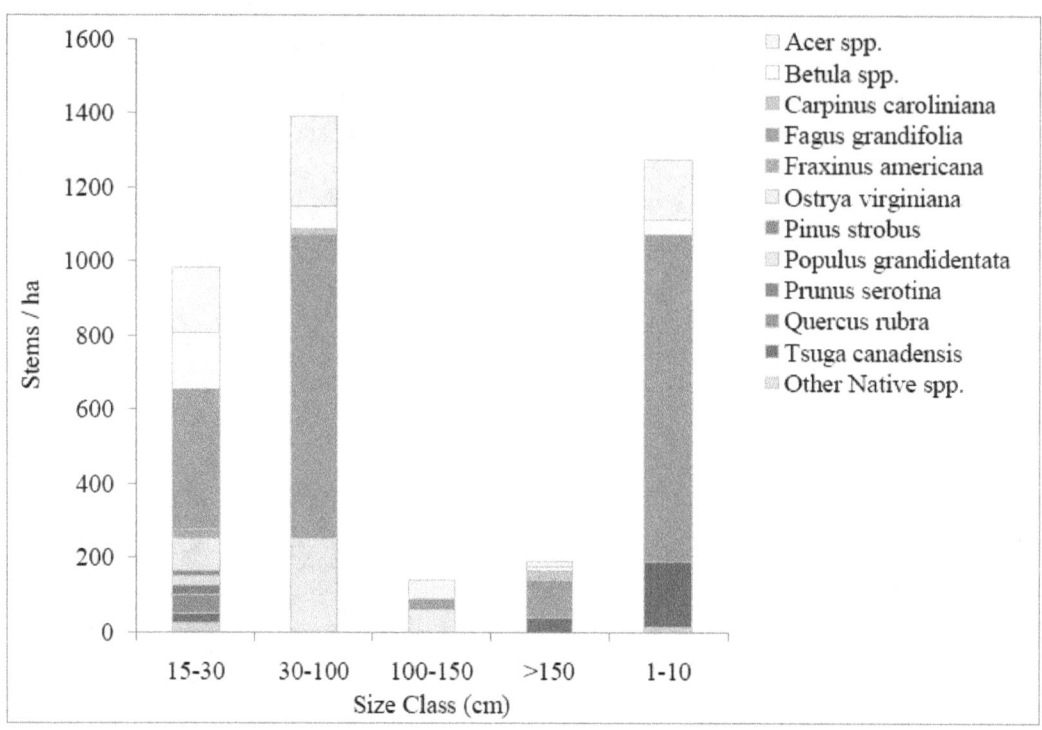

Figure F-8. Density of seedlings and saplings in Saint-Gaudens NHS. Classes 15-30, 30-100, 100-150 and >150cm (for individuals with diameter at breast height <1) reflect seedling height, and 1-10 DBH reflects sapling diameter at breast height.

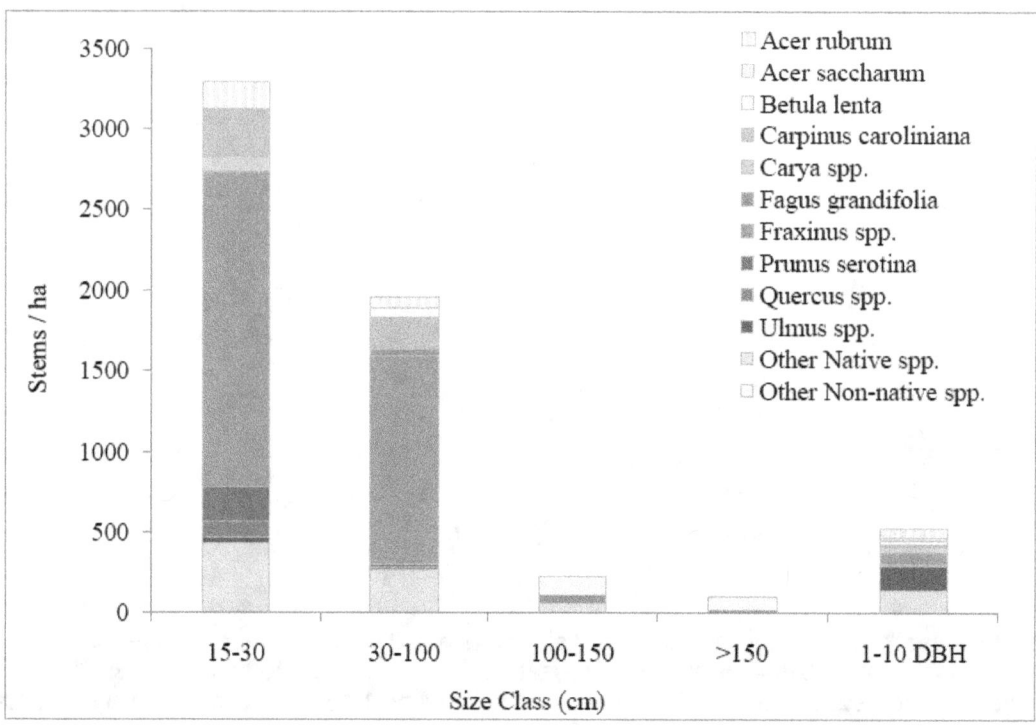

Figure F-9. Density of seedlings and saplings in Saratoga NHP. Classes 15-30, 30-100, 100-150 and >150cm (for individuals with diameter at breast height <1) reflect seedling height, and 1-10 DBH reflects sapling diameter at breast height.

Appendix F. Seedling and sapling density graphs (continued)

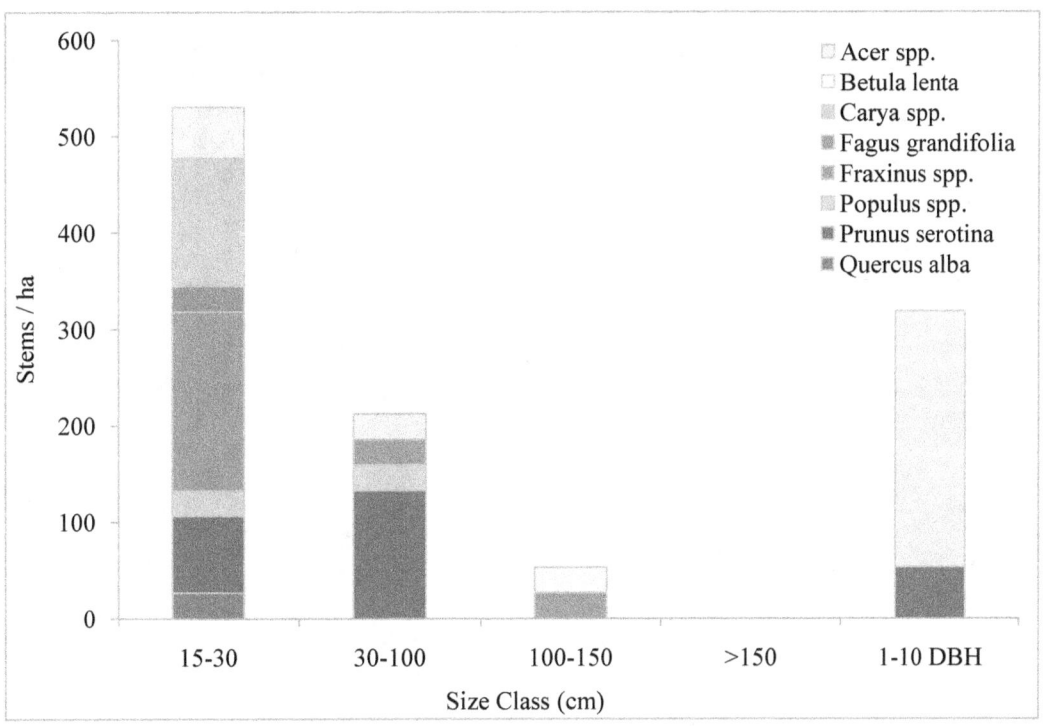

Figure F-10. Density of seedlings and saplings in Weir Farm NHS. Classes 15-30, 30-100, 100-150 and > 150cm (for individuals with diameter at breast height < 1) reflect seedling height, and 1-10 DBH reflects sapling diameter at breast height.

June 2010